Byzantium: A Very Short Introduction

T0058754

VERY SHORT INTRODUCTIONS are for anyone wanting a stimulating and accessible way into a new subject. They are written by experts, and have been translated into more than 45 different languages.

The series began in 1995, and now covers a wide variety of topics in every discipline. The VSI library now contains over 500 volumes—a Very Short Introduction to everything from Psychology and Philosophy of Science to American History and Relativity—and continues to grow in every subject area.

Titles in the series include the following:

Peter Sarris

BYZANTIUM

A Very Short Introduction

OXFORD
UNIVERSITY PRESS

Great Clarendon Street, Oxford, OX2 6DP,
United Kingdom

Oxford University Press is a department of the University of Oxford.
It furthers the University's objective of excellence in research, scholarship,
and education by publishing worldwide. Oxford is a registered trade mark of
Oxford University Press in the UK and in certain other countries

© Peter Sarris 2015

The moral rights of the author have been asserted

First edition published in 2015

Published in the United States of America by Oxford University Press
198 Madison Avenue, New York, NY 10016, United States of America

British Library Cataloguing in Publication Data
Data available

Library of Congress Control Number: 2015931306

ISBN 978-0-19-923611-4

Printed and bound by CPI Group (UK) Ltd, Croydon, CR0 4YY

For T.F.S. with love

Contents

Preface

This book was completed over the course of a Summer Fellowship at the Dumbarton Oaks Research Library in Washington, DC, whilst I was otherwise working on a study of the 'Novels' of the Emperor Justinian. I would like to thank Margaret Mullett for her hospitality at Dumbarton Oaks (on this and a previous visit) as well as Deb Stewart and the other librarians for their assistance. My thanks also go to the Trustees of Harvard University for appointing me to the Fellowship, and to Jenny Nugee at OUP for her forbearance.

An early draft of this book benefited from the comments of Turlough Stone, to whom I am grateful. The understanding of Byzantium set out in the chapters that follow inevitably owes much to those who taught me Byzantine studies in Oxford (especially James Howard-Johnston, Cyril Mango, and Marlia Mundell Mango) as well as to the work of friends and colleagues such as (but not limited to) Mark Whittow, Catherine Holmes, Peter Frankopan, and Teresa Shawcross.

Much of the emphasis within this book is on warfare and its impact on Byzantine politics and culture. Byzantium was an empire, after all, which both lived by the sword and ultimately died by it. If the focus of this book dwells more on high culture than on economic structures, or fixes on the policies of emperors more often than it does on the lives of the peasantry, however, that is not because I regard such topics as unimportant, but rather because I address them in so much detail in my other writings.

Peter Sarris
Cambridge
2014

List of illustrations

List of maps

Chapter 1
What was Byzantium?

> The organic body sang together;
> Dialects of the world sprang in Byzantium;
> Back they rang to sing in Byzantium;
> The streets repeat the sound of the Throne
> > (Charles Williams, *The Vision of Empire*)

Faith, reason, and empire

Today, we live in a world in which religious fundamentalism of all sorts is on the rise, and in which the elevation of Reason above Faith, which was one of the great intellectual and cultural achievements of the 'Enlightenment' of the 18th century, finds itself increasingly contested and publicly challenged. Some exponents of fundamentalist religion even reject the fruits of modern science and technology, regarding them as morally corrupting. Thus, in the old town of Jerusalem, walls are plastered with posters in Hebrew denouncing those who use the Internet or who are seen with smartphones. Yet many others (especially Islamic fundamentalists) have seized the opportunities offered by science (above all modern communications technology) to spread their message and press their case. Science is thereby harnessed to the cause of what they regard as true religion.

Those who view the world from a secularist perspective may regard such a position as incongruous, but it is in fact the opposition that the Enlightenment set up between Reason and Faith that is, in a sense, the historical anomaly. Nothing encapsulates this more clearly than the history of the Christian Empire, ruled for over a thousand years from the great city of Constantinople, that we know as Byzantium.

In terms of the official ideology and propaganda of those who ruled over it, Byzantium was not just a fundamentally Christian society, presided over by an emperor who was God's representative on earth. The empire was also believed by many to form a central part of God's divine dispensation for mankind. Understood in mystical terms, the earthly empire that emanated from Constantinople blended, merged, and united with the heavenly kingdom of Christ.

In that sense, it was a more profoundly religious society in terms of its core ideology than any of the other societies, kingdoms, and empires around it. In Byzantium, some claimed, heaven and earth were one. Yet, at the same time, it was the technologically and scientifically most advanced of the powers of the western Eurasian world in the early Middle Ages, one which was able to terrify Muslim attackers with its secret weapon of 'Greek fire' (probably a petroleum-based compound which was squirted through siphons and set ablaze to destroy enemy ships and men) and which could astound visitors from the Latin West with the great mechanical devices that adorned public spaces in the capital and surrounded the emperor in his court.

It was, of course, precisely because Byzantium was represented as so fundamentally religious a society that the writers and thinkers of the Enlightenment were so dismissive of it, and it was because of their dismissal that until comparatively recently the history of Byzantium has been so neglected in schools and universities.

To Edward Gibbon, whose *Decline and Fall of the Roman Empire* was to make such an imprint on the educated Anglophone mind, Byzantine history was 'a tedious and uniform tale of weakness and misery'. 'On the throne, in the camp, in the schools,' he declared, 'we search perhaps with fruitless diligence, the names and characters that deserve to be rescued from oblivion.' To Voltaire, it was 'a worthless collection of orations and miracles...a disgrace to the human mind'. His fellow Frenchman Montesquieu concurred, describing the complicated politics of the empire as 'nothing but a tissue of rebellions, sedition and treachery'.

It is to Montesquieu that we owe the usage of the term 'Byzantine' to refer to chronic bureaucratic complexity, interminable intrigue, and endemic corruption. The German high priest of reason, Hegel, was no less critical, informing his reader of the history of the empire that 'its general aspect presents a disgusting picture of imbecility; wretched, even insane, passions stifle the growth of all that is noble in thoughts, deeds and persons'. Politically despotic and deeply pietistic, Holy Byzantium was represented as a prison of the intellect and the soul. As a result, Byzantium's intellectual and scientific achievements were dismissed, and signs that it possessed a more diverse religious culture than its official ideology sanctioned were ignored.

Even those Romantic authors and mystical poets, such as W. B. Yeats and Charles Williams, who were drawn to the culture of Byzantium in the 19th and 20th centuries, were attracted to it precisely *because* of its supposed sidelining of Reason and its associated elevation of the sublime. It was, perhaps, a small blessing to a much maligned civilization that Sir Walter Scott never got round to finishing his Byzantine novel set at the time of the Crusades, *Count Robert of Paris*. It was one of the most turgid of his works (although, it must be admitted, he was writing it having been trepanned).

In the pages that follow, we shall see that Byzantium was a far more complex culture and society than either its Enlightenment critics or its Romantic devotees were willing to admit, and it is precisely this complexity that makes it so fascinating. Byzantium was a Christian society in which monks and churchmen as well as Christian laymen preserved the fruits of classical Greek (and pagan) philosophy, literature, and learning. Because of this, it would always generate individuals who, through their reading, would come to prefer Homer to Christ, or Plato to St Paul.

It was a culture that was inclined to eschew innovation, but which blended subject peoples of such diverse origins that it could not help but spawn many new literary, artistic, and architectural styles and forms. It was a world power which for centuries was locked in conflict with the Islamic world, but which learned to live alongside and deal with its neighbour pragmatically and subtly, avoiding much of the demonization of the 'other' that would characterize many Latin and western responses to the Muslim east. It was also an economy which, for many centuries, preserved much of the economic sophistication of antiquity which western Europe lost in the 5th century with the demise of Roman control.

Above all, it was a civilization from which no one modern nation state or polity can claim to be descended, or on whose legacy no one people can claim a monopoly. Not just Greeks but Turks, not just Russians and Serbians but many Armenians, Georgians, Syrians, and others can all claim, in different ways (and to differing degrees) to be heirs to the Empire of Byzantium or aspects of its legacy.

Why 'Byzantium'?

'The Christian Empire that we know as Byzantium' is how the Byzantine Empire was described in the preceding section. That is because very few of those who lived in the empire ever described themselves as 'Byzantine'. The adjective *Byzantinos* was sometimes used to describe individuals from the city of Constantinople, which had been known in Greek as *Byzantion* until the Emperor Constantine chose to rename the settlement in his own honour (*Konstantinoupolis Nea Romê*—'the city of Constantine the New Rome') in AD 325.

Even that usage of 'Byzantine', however, was largely a literary affectation. The term 'Byzantine' was borrowed in the 16th century by the German classical scholar Hieronymus Wolf (1516–80), who used it to describe a number of Greek-language authors who wrote on imperial affairs. It was kept in currency in the 17th century by scholars at the court of the French kings Louis XIII and Louis XIV, who lent their patronage to the publication of a number of 'Byzantine' Greek texts. Thereafter the label stuck, although some modern scholars of Byzantium prefer to describe the empire and its civilization as 'East Roman'.

This is for the very good reason that all 'Byzantine' emperors, and many of their subjects, always regarded themselves as Roman, and the empire in which they lived as the direct continuation of the Roman Empire of Augustus and Marcus Aurelius. Byzantium was not 'heir' to Rome—it *was* Rome. In Greek, they called themselves 'Romans' (*Rhomaioi*) just as modern Turks still refer to many Greek-speaking Christians (such as those in Cyprus, and the final remnants of the Greek community in Istanbul) not as Greeks but as *Rum*. In their own imagination, they were every bit as Roman as Livy and Cicero. In order to understand why, we have to go back to a series of struggles for power that almost ripped apart the Roman world in the 3rd and 4th centuries AD. In particular, we must look to the figure of the Emperor Constantine and his dynasty.

From Diocletian to Constantine

By the start of the 3rd century AD, the Roman Empire had expanded from the city of Rome to embrace a vast swathe of territory and a diverse body of subject peoples, from Britain in the west to Syria in the east, and from the River Danube in the north to the distant reaches of Upper Egypt and the Atlas Mountains in the

Byzantium

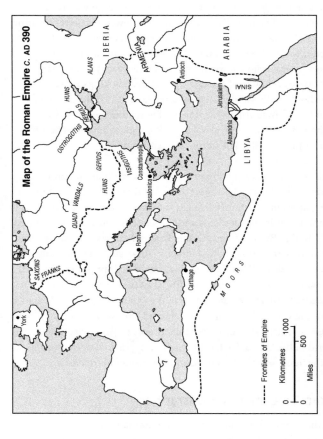

Map 1. The Roman Empire c. 390.

south (see Map 1). This the Romans had achieved through brilliant feats of arms, great diplomatic cunning, and the careful nurturing and reconciliation of the ambitions and expectations of the locally powerful in those regions over which the Romans aspired to extend their control. Those who were willing to co-operate with Rome, and buy into its values and culture, were granted status, honour, and rank, and were entrusted with much of the day-to-day governance and administration of the territories in which they lived.

The world that the Roman Empire created through its efforts was fundamentally city-based. That is to say, the regional elites who were co-opted into the project of empire lived in monumental urban centres termed *civitates* in Latin, or *poleis* in Greek. There, they were organized into city councils styled *curiae* or *boulai*. It was primarily through these city councils that the emperor ruled—his will being mediated to the councillors via imperially appointed governors, who, in turn, reported back to the emperor and senate of Rome on the condition of the provinces. Such a relatively devolved system facilitated rule over the enormous area of the empire, although the highest offices of state remained the preserve of a markedly conservative, Italian-rooted senatorial order focused on the city of Rome.

This system came under great pressure in the mid-3rd century AD. Economic and political contact between Rome and the various barbarian peoples beyond the Rhine and the Danube to the north undermined the latters' native and relatively egalitarian social structures, and led to the emergence among them of ever larger tribes and confederations, who were better able to challenge Roman mastery of the frontier zone.

At the same time, the closing years of the 2nd century had seen the Roman Empire extend its eastern frontier at the expense of the Persians. This defeat at the hands of Rome led to the downfall of the ruling Arsacid dynasty, and—following a struggle in which different aristocratic interests vied for ascendancy—its replacement at the head of the Persian world by the Sasanian dynasty.

In September 226, at the palace of Ctesiphon, the first Sasanian Shah Ardashir was crowned. Ardashir soon sought to unite the aristocracy of Persia behind him by launching a series of prestige-garnering offensives against the Romans. This policy of aggression was followed by his son and successor Shapur I, who, in 260, launched a daring campaign into northern Syria, sacking Antioch, and capturing and humiliating the Emperor Valerian.

In response to this crisis, a social revolution took place. The emperor, hitherto appointed by the senate in Rome, came increasingly to be appointed by the army. Not unnaturally, the army began to appoint men from its own ranks. The result was a series of military emperors of humble origin, absolutely committed to the ideology of empire but impatient of failure. This process culminated in 284 in the figure of Diocletian, who overcame his rivals, established himself as emperor, and waged a series of successful campaigns against foes internal and external alike.

The peace that Diocletian restored to the empire gave him the opportunity to consolidate a series of administrative reforms. A system of power sharing was introduced to give the empire more devolved leadership closer to the likely sources of military threat. This would eventually take the form of the 'Tetrarchy' (or 'rule of four'), whereby the empire was divided between two *Augusti* or emperors—one to face down enemies in the east, and one to confront those in the west—to each of whom was also appointed a deputy or *Caesar*. These *supremos* of imperial power resided in imperial capitals nearer the frontiers of the empire, such as Trier in the west, or Antioch to the east.

At the same time, the administrative and fiscal system was restructured to facilitate greater imperial control of provincial life. Military and civilian commands in the provinces were separated, and the size of the army increased. The provinces were reduced in size and increased in number so as to tighten central supervision of the city councils.

As a result of the expansion of the army, and an enlargement of the overarching imperial bureaucracy, the number of high-ranking military and civilian officials directly employed by the central imperial government appears to have more than doubled. These officials were primarily recruited from among the dominant elements within the provincial city councils of the empire. Alongside these changes, membership of the senatorial order was increasingly opened up to them.

A new imperial aristocracy of service thus emerged and began to dominate imperial politics. Crucially, this reconfiguration of power in the Roman world led to a shift of power and influence to the empire's primarily Greek-speaking eastern provinces, where the senior emperor ultimately resided, in order to keep a careful eye on Rome's great superpower rival—the newly belligerent Persian Empire.

This fact would have increasingly marked implications for the political culture of the Roman Empire and, in particular, the behaviour and deportment of emperors and those who surrounded them. Until the political ascendancy of Julius Caesar's adoptive son, Octavian, who defeated his rival Mark Antony in 31 BC, the Roman Empire had been a republic, theoretically ruled by the Senate and People of Rome.

It was Octavian (taking up the title *Augustus*—meaning something like 'venerable' or 'superhuman') who first established himself as emperor. However, Octavian had left the republican institutions of the Roman constitution intact beneath his own overarching authority, and presented the imperial office as a sort of conglomeration of republican offices. Thus he depicted himself not as overlord of the Roman world (which he really was) but rather

Chief Magistrate of the Roman Republic. It was in these republican terms that the imperial office was initially understood in much of the empire's Latin-speaking western provinces, where the local elites had learned and acquired their political culture from Rome.

In the primarily Greek-speaking eastern provinces of the empire, by contrast, the political culture was very different. With the exception of Greece itself, these were territories that had once been ruled over by the great monarchies of Persia and Egypt, whose kings had been lionized as gods. These rulers in turn had typically regarded their subjects as little better than proverbial (or actual) slaves. The deeply engrained culture of divine monarchy in these regions had essentially been preserved in the 4th century BC, when these lands had been conquered by the fiery genius of Alexander the Great of Macedon, who took little convincing that he too was a god.

Although Alexander and his heirs had been able to Hellenize the local elites of Egypt, Syria, and Palestine, imparting to them the Greek language and Greek intellectual culture, the style of rule adopted by the Macedonian kings was necessarily shaped to meet local expectations. Their political vocabulary of divine monarchy had been passed on to the Romans as Roman power in turn had expanded eastwards.

In the great city of Ephesus, for example, inscriptions honouring emperors in Latin accorded them such republican titles as *Pontifex Maximus* (meaning high priest of the college of pontiffs in Rome), while declaring the emperor in Greek to be the *autokrator*, or 'sole ruler'. Elsewhere in the east, the emperor was described as the *kosmokrator* ('world-ruler') and his freeborn Roman subjects as his *douloi* ('slaves').

There was a natural tendency for the political culture of Rome's Greek-speaking eastern provinces to radiate westwards. But the influence of that culture was reinforced and intensified by the institution of the Tetrarchy, and Diocletian's decision to base himself in the east. For it meant that the senior emperor was operating in a political context in which the tradition of divine monarchy was at its strongest, and where, for him to project his power effectively, he had to project it in such terms.

As a near contemporary, Aurelius Victor, declared of Diocletian:

> He was a great man, but with the following habits: he was the first to want a robe woven with gold, and sandals with plenty of silk, purple, and jewels; although this exceeded humility and revealed a swollen and arrogant mind, it was nothing compared to the rest, for he was the first of all the emperors after Caligula and Domitian to allow himself to be called 'master' [Latin *dominus*] in public, to be worshipped and addressed as a god.

The imperial office had thus become both militarized and highly ceremonialized, with the emperor increasingly depicted as the representation of divinity on earth. Diocletian, in particular, claimed to hold authority from Jupiter, the father of the gods in the Roman pantheon, who was depicted as the emperor's divine companion.

In the year 305, the elderly Diocletian did something remarkable for a Roman emperor: he retired, together with the junior *Augustus* Maximian. Diocletian was succeeded by his deputy, Galerius, in the east, and in the west power passed to the *Caesar* Constantius. In 306, however, as he marched through the province of Britain to police its troublesome northern frontier, the Emperor Constantius died at York. Instead of acknowledging Constantius' *Caesar*, Severus, as the new western *Augustus*, however, the field army in Britain threw its support behind the late Constantius' son, the young prince Constantine (Figure 1).

A new round of civil war and infighting thus ensued, as different factions and armies threw their weight behind rival claimants to

1. Marble head of Constantine, now in the Capitoline Museum, Rome.

imperial power. One by one, however, Constantine eliminated these rivals. In 312, he secured his ascendancy in the west by prising the city of Rome from the grip of Maximian's son, Maxentius, whom he defeated at the Battle of the Milvian Bridge. In 323, he marched east to face down the last of his foes, Licinius, whom he defeated on land and then, in 324, at sea, in the near vicinity of the ancient Greek settlement of Byzantion (Latin, *Byzantium*), built on the straits of the Bosphorus that linked Europe to Asia.

In celebration of his victory, as we have seen, he renamed the city *Konstantinoupolis Nea Romê*—'Constantinople the New Rome'—the following year. Constantine was now the sole master of the entire Roman world, over which he presided from his new city.

A new religion

As his dedication to the father of the gods, Jupiter, reveals, Diocletian was something of a conservative in matters of religion, and his reign had witnessed the persecution of followers of what he regarded as alien cults, whose presence within the empire he regarded as a source of divine displeasure. Among those who most attracted his opprobrium were Christians. These were followers of an offshoot and mutation of the ancestral faith of the empire's Jewish subjects.

Christians advocated the exclusive worship of what they regarded as the one 'true' God, whose son, it was claimed, had been made man in the form of an itinerant Palestinian preacher known as Jesus Christ (Greek, *Christos*—'the anointed one'), who had been executed by the Roman authorities under the Emperor Tiberius. Like the Jews, these Christians refused to sacrifice to the imperial cult (an obligation incumbent upon all the emperor's subjects).

To Romans of a traditional frame of mind, the Jews could be forgiven this: their refusal to sacrifice was justified on the grounds that their ancestral religion forbade it, and theirs was a very ancient religion. Accordingly, the Jews were upholding the traditions of their ancestors, and this, to conservative Romans was a fundamentally virtuous thing to do. The Christians, however, could make no such claim, for theirs was a new religion. To many Romans, this would have been a contradiction in terms: a religion, almost by definition, needed to be ancient to be genuine.

We might imagine, therefore, that such people would have been shocked to hear that the new Emperor Constantine ascribed his stunning victory at the Battle of the Milvian Bridge in 312 to the fact that he too had become a devotee of the Christian God, a conversion that he later ascribed to a divinely ordained vision of a cross revealed to him in the heavens. Later, when entering Rome, Constantine refused to do what was expected of emperors, and sacrifice at the Altar of the Capitoline Jove. Instead, from 312 onwards he publicly declared his support for the Christian community or 'Church' (Greek, *ekklêsia*), favouring it and its priests with ever-greater largesse.

Constantine's conversion is often presented as a sudden and inexplicable event, one which was to alter inexorably the course of human history. In certain respects, however, Constantine's adoption of Christianity was perhaps less dramatic a break with the religious sensibilities of many of his 3rd-century predecessors than is sometimes supposed.

As we have seen with respect to Diocletian, emperors of the 3rd century had frequently and deliberately associated themselves with specific individual divine patrons or cults whose power they sought to tap. Traditional Roman religion was 'polytheistic' (meaning the Romans believed there were many gods). Such emperors thus possessed a great array of potential divine patrons to choose from.

The 2nd and 3rd centuries, however, witnessed the growing popularity not only of Christianity, which, like Judaism, was 'monotheistic' (meaning Christians believed there was only one God), but also of forms of 'henotheism' (advocating the belief that while there may be many deities, one should worship a single supreme God—from the Greek *henos* meaning 'one'). Henotheism seems to have been especially popular in military circles, and was typically associated with the worship of deities associated with the Sun, such as Mithras or *Sol Invictus* ('the Unconquered Sun').

By virtue of the rise to political dominance of military men over the course of the 3rd century, forms of solar henotheism had become an increasingly important and visible part of the public religious life of the Roman Empire. So, for example, both Diocletian's predecessor, Aurelian, and his successor in the west, Constantius I, were devotees of *Sol Invictus*, with whom they chose to associate themselves in their propaganda. Importantly, from an early date, Christianity seems to have circulated in very similar social circles as cults such as that of *Sol Invictus*, and was itself characterized by a strikingly solar imagery and vocabulary: in the New Testament, for example, Christ was described as 'the light of the world' or 'the day-spring'.

As a result, the line of demarcation between solar henotheism and monotheism with strong solar associations, was highly permeable, and it was out of this milieu that Constantine emerged. When this is taken into account, Constantine's religious migration around the year 312 from solar henotheism to Christianity was perhaps less dramatic than has appeared to posterity. Certainly, as late as 323, Constantine continued to mint coins dedicated to the 'divine companion the Unconquered Sun', and in Constantinople he erected a statue of himself as the sun-god Helios-Apollo. In his public imagery and propaganda, Constantine continued to use forms, expressions, and motifs which, while not exclusively 'pagan', could nevertheless appeal to a non-Christian audience while being read in an allegoricized Christian way by his co-devotees.

There may well have been an element of political pragmatism to this: Constantine had to be careful not to offend the powerful pagan elements within the governing classes of his empire, whose cooperation and support he needed. On the other hand, it may well be that the multivalent message of Constantine's public imagery itself accurately conveyed the nature of the emperor's own personal religiosity. At the same time, he conceived of his relationship to the Christian God just as rulers in the east had long thought of their relationship to the divine: he was God's 'vice-gerent' or deputy on earth. It was a belief that Christian courtiers were happy to accommodate: the influential eastern bishop Eusebius even addressed a speech to the emperor on the subject.

For twenty-five years from 312 until his death in 337, Constantine lent the Christian Church and its leaders concerted support. The same policy was pursued by his three sons (Constans I, Constantine II, and Constantius II) between whom the empire was divided after him. In 361 the imperial title passed briefly into the hands of the pagan Julian, but he reigned for little more than eighteen months, dying on campaign against the Persians.

As a result, at an official level the Roman state became evermore obviously and aggressively Christian, as emperors began to legislate to Christianize not only the public sphere (by constructing churches or banning public acts of pagan sacrifice), but also the domestic sphere (by seeking to prohibit long-established patterns of behaviour—most obviously marital and sexual—that the leaders of the Christian Church found objectionable).

Accordingly, many members of the Roman governing classes increasingly converted to Christianity in order to curry imperial favour. By the end of the 4th century, it would be clear that Christianity was not just the favoured cult of the emperor (as it had been under Constantine): it had metamorphosed into the official religion of the Roman state.

A new politics

Constantine's renaming of the city of Byzantium in his own honour was, as we have seen, a celebration of victory. But there was more to the foundation of Constantinople than mere self-glorification. The ancient Greek settlement of Byzantium, which Constantine expanded and embellished, offered certain advantages to its new ruler (although as we shall see in Chapter 2, it also presented numerous disadvantages).

It stood at a site of great natural beauty astride strong lines of maritime communication. Crucially, it was within reach of the disturbed Danubian and Persian frontiers. But perhaps most importantly of all, the establishment of a new power base in the east offered Constantine distinct and tangible political benefits that would help to consolidate his new regime.

Beyond the ranks of the Christian Church and clergy, he had no natural base of support in the east, and in Licinius he had deposed and murdered an emperor who had been popular among pagan and Christian alike. In the great cities of the east, hostility to the new regime may have been running high. The foundation of Constantinople had the advantage, therefore, of removing the person of the emperor from an alien and potentially threatening political environment. It enabled him to set about establishing his position in the east in a setting of his choosing and his creation.

At the same time, the creation of Constantinople and the eventual establishment there of a senate afforded Constantine and his dynasty the opportunity to begin to build up a network of well-born and influential clients, who could serve as his representatives, allies, and supporters in the new political conditions in which he found himself.

In order to entrench his political power in the east, it was vital that Constantine establish a personal following and affinity among the leading members of provincial society and the representatives of the new imperial aristocracy of service: the military 'top brass', the chief civil servants, and the proud and haughty landowners who dominated the city councils of the great eastern *metropoleis*. By beginning to draw such people to Constantinople, Constantine sought to co-opt them into his regime.

In order to attract men of influence to his new foundation, we thus see the emperor making grants of land to those building private residences in the city, and, in 332, instituting the regular distribution of bread rations derived from the rich corn supply of the fantastically fecund province of Egypt, which was shipped across the Mediterranean sea-lanes in vast quantities.

The foundation of Constantinople, and the subsequent establishment and expansion of its senate by Constantine's heirs (especially his son Constantius II—who accorded the Senate of Constantinople equal standing to that of Rome), played a vital part in legitimizing and stabilizing the new order.

The aim of this policy was clear: to establish the Constantinopolitan senate and its members as a real and effective point of contact between the imperial court and the provinces, where many of them owned land. The senators were to be the emperor's 'friends', his 'eyes and ears' in the world beyond the 'ruling city'. As the orator and bureaucrat Themistius put it to Constantius II in 350:

> For the emperor who must hear many things, see many things, and at the same time pay attention to many things, his two ears and his two eyes and his body... are very little indeed. But if he is rich in friends, he will see far and will hear things which are not close to him, and he will know what is far off—like the seers—and he will be present at the same time in many places—like a god.

Constantius II (337–61) needed little encouragement: he even granted and auctioned off extensive stretches of prime agricultural land to such people in order to lock them in to the regime. But most importantly, the long-term result of the policies adopted by Constantine and his dynasty would be to draw together members of the aristocracy of service of the eastern Mediterranean into a single political community, increasingly united by a sense of Roman political identity, Greek 'high culture', Christian faith, and, crucially, bound together by the Constantinopolitan focus of their political ambitions. It was this combination (forged in the 4th century) of Roman identity, Greek culture, Christian religion, and devotion to the city of Constantine that would define Byzantium and its civilization for over a thousand years.

Chapter 2
Constantinople the ruling city

Projecting power

Constantine's decision to rule from his new city of Constantinople did not immediately establish his foundation as the official capital of the Eastern Roman Empire. Into the late 4th century, imperial rule could be highly peripatetic, as emperors often travelled long distances to deal with their enemies and rivals in person. Constantine's son and successor in the east, Constantius II, for example, spent much of his time in the city of Antioch in Syria, from where he coordinated efforts to contain the Persian threat. In 357, Constantius also visited Rome, where his resolutely autocratic style and military demeanour left a lasting impression on the crowds who flocked to see him. The contemporary historian Ammianus Marcellinus, for example, recorded the emperor's formal entry (*adventus*) into the city, in a description that epitomizes the style of rule to which the eastern provincials had long been accustomed: 'And it was as if he were planning to overawe the Euphrates with a show of force,' Ammianus writes, 'while the standards preceded him on either side, he himself stood alone upon a golden chariot in the resplendent blaze of various precious stones, whose mingled glitter seemed to form a sort of second daylight.'

Only from the reign of Theodosius I (378–95) was Constantinople accorded the formal status of the sole imperial capital in the east and permanent imperial residence, and in the 6th century the Emperor Justinian (527–65) would refer to it in his laws as the 'ruling city' or the 'queen of cities'. All emperors from Constantine to Justinian, however, invested in the city and contributed to its remarkable architectural development, which transformed it from the small provincial town it had once been, into the supreme stage for the projection of imperial power.

The original Byzantion, like most traditional Greek cities, was focused on its *acropolis*, set on the eastern promontory overlooking the Golden Horn. Next to the acropolis stood the *forum* or *agora*, where much of the town's commercial life had been concentrated. There was also an amphitheatre for gladiatorial and other games.

Constantine and his heirs, however, fundamentally reorientated the city by building a palace complex to the south of the acropolis, which effectively became the city's new beating heart. Adjacent to the palace complex were built the Senate House, the Cathedral Church of Hagia Sophia or 'Holy Wisdom', the imperial basilica where much of the city's legal life would be conducted, a large public bath (the 'Baths of Zeuxippus'), and, crucially, the Hippodrome, where the emperor presided over chariot races for the entertainment of the city's populace.

All of these faced on to a large public square called the *Augustaeum*. The juxtaposition of palace, cathedral, and Hippodrome, in particular, facilitated an intricate interweaving of public and private secular and religious ceremonial activities that would determine the rhythm of the life of the city for centuries to come.

To the west of the *Augustaeum* was the golden milestone (*milion*), from where all distances within the empire were reckoned. Beyond it stretched the main processional route known as the *mese* (or 'middle road') that led through the Forum of Constantine (one of the numerous public squares adorned with statues and monuments with which the city was dotted) to the Capitol. In the middle of the Forum of Constantine stood a porphyry column bearing a bronze statue of the emperor. At the Capitol the road split: to the north-west it extended out to the Constantinian walls of the city, passing the Church of the Holy Apostles that Constantine had ordered to be built as an imperial mausoleum, while the more westerly branch of the road linked the Capitol to the 'Golden Gate', which was the main and formal point of entry into the city (see Map 2).

Again, this effectively created a stage on which ceremonial processions (such as Constantius II's *adventus* into Rome in 357) could be performed, allowing the emperor and his entourage to engage in a display of imperial power while also receiving the acclamations and praise (and sometimes complaints) of his subjects. More so than any other city in the Roman Empire, Constantinople was designed to convey and articulate imperial authority. As a result, it arguably resembled the great 'palace cities' of the Far and Middle East more than it did traditional forms of Greek or Roman urbanism.

Architecturally, the main principle of Constantine's city was predicated upon straight colonnaded streets punctuated by squares. In this respect it had much in common with other eastern cities, such as Antioch, Apamea, or Palmyra in Syria. Where it surpassed all other cities, however, was in terms of the richness with which those squares and other public spaces were decorated, with monuments and objects gathered (or ransacked) from throughout the empire. Constantine, for example, adorned the Baths of Zeuxippus (which were a venue not just for bathing but also for public speaking and debate) with statues in marble and bronze, including three statues of Apollo, three of Aphrodite, two of Heracles, and one of Poseidon, along with twenty-nine statues of characters connected to the Trojan legend (such as Helen, Andromache, and Aeneas). Constantine decorated the

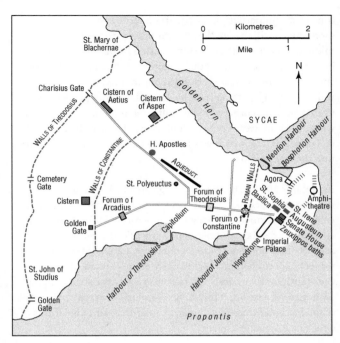

Map 2. Plan of Constantinople.

Hippodrome with further statues of pagan deities, wild animals, and legendary creatures such as sphinxes. Perhaps most importantly, he placed there two monuments associated with military triumph: a statue celebrating Octavian's defeat of Mark Antony at the Battle of Actium, and the Serpent Column from Delphi dedicated to the Greek allies who had defeated the Persians in 479 BC at the Battle of Platea. The Hippodrome was also festooned with images of Alexander the Great, Julius Caesar, and the emperors Augustus and Diocletian. In the Forum of Constantine, the statue of the emperor kept company with a statue of Pallas Athena which was brought from Rome, and other statues on mythological and literary themes.

Sporadic attempts were also made to give Constantinople something of the air of the older Rome. In particular, the Emperor Theodosius I (who claimed descent from the Emperor Trajan) created a reproduction of Trajan's forum in Rome, while his son Theodosius II (408–50) added to Constantinople's six existing hills a seventh (on the model of the city on the Tiber). There are also hints in the sources that houses built for members of the aristocracy replicated Roman architectural and decorative schemes: one 10th-century account, for example, noted of these 4th-century palaces that 'if one beheld their entrance halls and courtyards and staircases, how similar they were in the scale of their design and height to those in Rome, and if one beheld their doors, one seemed in one's imagination to be in Rome'.

At the same time, however, Theodosius I also placed in the Hippodrome a magnificent obelisk from Alexandria, and as more members of the provincial governing classes were drawn to the city, they too are likely to have brought with them their own architectural and artistic tastes that can only have added to the city's already eclectic feel.

In the early 6th century, for example, the fantastically wealthy Roman aristocrat Anicia Iuliana built between the Capitol and the Church of Holy Apostles her own church dedicated to St Polyeuktos. It would seem that, in its style, this church (which no longer stands) was meant to evoke the Temple of Solomon, and drew upon an architectural repertoire of Egyptian origin. As an international centre of political power, the monumental appearance of Constantinople as it took shape between the 4th and 6th centuries was truly (and appropriately) cosmopolitan.

If the blend of architectural and artistic styles that came to characterize the city of Constantinople was unique, so too were certain of the techniques adopted by the city's builders and artisans. While, as we have seen, the location of the ancient Greek settlement of Byzantium possessed many natural advantages, one of its great disadvantages was that it lay on a seismic fault line, and was thus vulnerable to earthquakes.

This almost certainly explains certain oddities of the city's architecture. Compared to traditional Roman building practices, for example, the builders of Constantinople used a much higher ratio of mortar to brick in their constructions (typically something in the order of 2:1). They also built on barrelled vaults, sometimes lining the dead spaces above the springing of the vaults with earthenware jars. Such techniques would have served to give buildings greater structural flexibility in the face of earthquakes, and thus a greater chance of surviving seismic shocks. The structural emphasis on mortar, however, could also make for a rather drab external appearance, thereby giving Byzantine artisans, donors, and patrons an incentive to concentrate instead on the internal splendour and decorative schemes of their architectural projects.

Constantine's city also possessed two further locational disadvantages with which the emperors of the 4th to 6th centuries had to deal. The first was that although the tidal peculiarities of the Bosphorus made the city very hard to attack successfully by sea, it was highly vulnerable to a land assault from the European side and the plains of Thrace. In particular, there were no natural defences to get in the way of any invader advancing from the near side of the Danube or the Crimean Steppe.

The turbulence within the northern barbarian world caused by the rise of the Huns in the late 4th and early 5th centuries thus obliged the imperial authorities to take this matter in hand, and between 404 and 413 the Emperor Theodosius II oversaw the construction of a massive set of triple-level defences (comprising an inner wall, an outer wall, and a moat). These 'Theodosian walls' (much of which still stand, see Figure 2) represented the acme of Roman military engineering, and would prove to be impregnable until the advent of modernity and the invention of gunpowder. An

2. The triple-level Theodosian Walls of Constantinople.

additional set of defences (known as the 'Anastasian' or 'Long Walls') would be added in the late 5th and early 6th centuries, although these proved to be too long for the authorities to be able to man.

It was evidently decided that the Theodosian walls should encompass a considerably greater area of land than had the original Constantinian ones. This decision was probably taken in part with a view to accommodating the city's teeming population, which by the early 5th century may well have outgrown the confines of the Constantinian foundation.

It should be noted, however, that much of the land between the Constantinian walls and the Theodosian ones was, from the very start, turned over to agriculture, thus enabling the city's population to at least attempt to feed itself when besieged. In normal times, much of the population of the city received a free 'dole' of bread, wine, and oil. The bread, as we have seen, was made with grain shipped to Constantinople from Egypt (the East

Roman world's most agriculturally productive region, and thus the 'bread basket' of empire).

The final significant locational disadvantage from which the city of Constantinople suffered (and which besets the modern city of Istanbul to this day) was one of water supply. The city and its immediate environs possessed very little by way of sources of fresh water for drinking and bathing. As a result, gargantuan efforts were made to build an enormous series of aqueducts which snaked out across the Thracian landscape for over 200 kilometres to the west.

Such aqueducts, of course, were highly vulnerable to attack (the Aqueduct of Valens, for example, was deliberately cut off by the Avars when they laid siege to the city in 626). Emperors attempted to remedy this by building a remarkable network of underground and open-air cisterns in which to maintain reserves. The three open-air cisterns built between the Theodosian and Constantinian walls, for example, had a combined capacity of almost one million cubic metres, while the underground cisterns such as Justinian's 'cisterna basilica' or the cistern of Philoxenos (between the Hippodrome and the Forum of Constantine) remain to this day among the most stunning remains of Byzantine Constantinople.

From an early date the city also had a relatively clearly defined social geography, with the houses of the aristocracy, such as those described earlier, and 'grace and favour' residences owned by the crown and issued to the emperor's relatives and favourites, concentrated around the palace complex and to the west of the city (with the more rural zone between the Theodosian and Constantinian walls being particularly well suited to suburban villas).

In general terms, most housing for the ordinary population appears to be have been concentrated to the north-west, near the main commercial zone focused on the Neorion harbour on the Golden Horn, where most wholesale goods were brought in.

To the south of the city, two large artificial harbours were added over the course of the 4th century: the so-called harbour of Julian and the Theodosian harbour. These appear to have been primarily designed to accommodate the ships carrying grain to Constantinople from Egypt, and near the harbours large silos were built to house the grain. The larger the city grew, the more vital such supplies became.

Constantinople probably reached its peak of population in the early 6th century under the Emperor Justinian, when it was conceivably home to some 500,000 inhabitants. Certainly, Justinian complained of the problems caused in the city by migration from the countryside, and concerted attempts were made to introduce population controls. In 542, however, fate intervened, and the city (along with the rest of the empire) was struck by the first known outbreak of bubonic plague. The contemporary historian Procopius was present in Constantinople when the plague first struck, and he describes how at one point it wiped out 10,000 victims in a single day. He also records the digging of mass graves beyond the city walls, and the disposal of corpses in the sea by the Golden Horn, where the currents would have trapped them to rot.

This would have made life for the survivors around the Neorion harbour and the commercial district extremely unpleasant (especially given the contemporary belief that disease was caused by 'bad air'). It should not surprise us, therefore, that from around the middle of the 6th century we see signs of a shift of population to the south of the city, and the development of the harbour of Julian as a new commercial centre. The Neorion, by contrast, became a naval dockyard, and the Golden Horn would not recover its economic significance until Italian merchants negotiated the right to found trading colonies there in the 11th century.

The 6th century also witnessed the final phase in the architectural development of what we might term the 'antique city', driven by political events. The Hippodrome, as we have seen, stood in the political heart of the capital, and the fans who thronged the races and games were divided into four circus 'factions', of which the two most popular were the Blues and the Greens.

These factions were accorded a significant role in the ceremonial life of the city, participating, for example, in imperial coronations, where they represented the voice of 'the people'. They also had certain civic responsibilities and duties delegated to them, such as fire fighting, or helping to man the city walls in event of enemy attack. At the same time, however, they were capable of causing great disruption, not least by periodically engaging in bouts of inter-factional violence and rioting.

Procopius, in his *Secret History*, paints a vivid picture of the lawlessness of the faction members, which included rape, abduction, fashion muggings, and murder. He also describes their outlandish 'Hunnic' hairstyle: cropped at the sides, long on top, and with a 'mullet' at the back. The factions included youths of all classes, and their rioting could be turned to political purposes (especially in return for cash).

In response to a renewed outbreak of inter-factional rioting, in the year 532 the Emperor Justinian had the leaders of the Blue and Green factions arrested. This led the factions to unite against him, in an upsurge of violence which Justinian's opponents in the senate attempted to exploit in order to have the emperor deposed.

Justinian considered taking flight, but was dissuaded by his wife, the indomitable Empress Theodora, who had previously been an actress, and whom Procopius (who hated Justinian) describes as a meddlesome whore. His nerves steeled by his wife, Justinian mobilized his supporters in the army against the mob, and 30,000 rioters are reported to have been cut down in the Hippodrome. Justinian also seized the opportunity to move against his enemies in the senate, thereby consolidating his fragile regime.

The 'Nika' riots as they are known (after the chant of the marauding mob—*Nika!*—'conquer!') not only failed to depose the emperor, but also managed to inflict massive harm on the monumental centre of the capital: the rioters reduced Hagia Sophia to ashes, as well as the nearby church of St Irene, the offices of the Praetorian Prefecture of the East (where, usefully, criminal records and other such documents are likely to have been kept), and many of the others buildings of state around the *Augustaeum*. Significantly, in the wake of the Nika riots, Justinian seized the moment and rebuilt the monumental heart of the city in a spectacular feat of self-glorification, epitomized by his audacious (albeit somewhat slap-dash) rebuilding of Hagia Sophia.

Prior to the rioting, Justinian had commissioned the building of a new church to the south of the palace complex dedicated to the Syrian saints Sergius and Bacchus. This church was meant to serve as a home for Syrian monks and clergy in the city, who attracted the patronage of the Empress Theodora. In Syria there existed a tradition of domed ecclesiastical architecture, and perhaps by way of an allusion and *homage* to the homeland of Theodora's clients, the Church of SS Sergius and Bacchus was planned and constructed around a central dome. Although it was built a little off-square, it turned out to be a construction of striking elegance and charm, the conception of which may well have inspired Justinian and his architects to choose to reconstruct Hagia Sophia on similar principles (in place of the basilica church which had stood there before), albeit on a massively larger scale (see Figure 3).

Like SS Sergius and Bacchus, Hagia Sophia was built as a domed church. Within a rectangle of 70 × 76 metres, four enormous pillars were positioned to form a square with sides of 30 metres. These pillars supported pendentives 20 metres from the ground, which in turn supported the enormous central dome 30 metres in diameter, soaring to a height of 52 metres.

3. Exterior view of Hagia Sophia with Turkish minarets.

Beyond the central dome-in-square were erected further walls, piers, and columns to support the external walls and provide additional aisles and arcades.

The lower parts of the church were dressed with marble: grey marble paving slabs on the floor, with multicoloured marble on the lower structures. The upper arcades and aisles, by contrast, were decorated with a finely wrought display of carved marble, while the upper walls were adorned with a glittering array of mosaic cubes illuminated by the light shining in through the coloured glass windows, thereby leading the eye (and the mind) upwards to the contemplation of the divine mysteries.

Justinian's Hagia Sophia was constructed remarkably quickly: barely five years elapsed between the Nika riots and its formal inauguration. This necessarily meant that it was something of a rushed job: the empire, for example, had been ransacked for building materials for the project, yet the architects were unable to find enough pillars that matched in terms of size and material

30

to avoid giving it a slightly hotchpotch appearance. Likewise, the vast expanse of patterned mosaics that covered the upper walls were probably deployed because they were cheaper to make and quicker to install than the more elaborate figuratively decorated mosaic alternatives. In the central pendentives, however, were placed four remarkably vivid and palpably potent mosaic images (which have only been uncovered relatively recently), perhaps depicting archangels or similar heavenly powers.

Yet, however hastily executed, the reconstruction of Hagia Sophia was a triumph of both structural and lighting engineering. 'Solomon,' Justinian is reported to have exclaimed upon its completion, 'I have beaten you!' In the 10th century, visitors to Constantinople from the Scandinavian and Slav settlement of Kiev would choose to be baptized into the Orthodox Christian faith of the emperor on the grounds that, in Hagia Sophia, they believed they had seen where God truly dwelled.

The medieval city

The city of Constantinople as visitors would encounter it for most of the Middle Ages was essentially the city as it was left by Justinian. This was partly because no emperor after Justinian would have the economic resources required to build on the scale or with the ambition that the emperors of late antiquity had done. To the medieval and Byzantine imagination, the 'Ruling City' would be characterized by the two greatest features of its late antique landscape: Hagia Sophia and the Theodosian walls. Indeed, images of a dome in a castle almost became a visual shorthand for the city.

The main change that occurred in the years immediately following Justinian's reign is that the Christian character of the city became increasingly pronounced, as new churches proliferated within its walls, relics of the saints from throughout the Christian world were brought to it and, in particular, as a tradition developed that the city of Constantine had been placed under the divine protection of the Mother of God.

This tradition probably originated in the 5th century when a series of Theodosian empresses had encouraged and developed the cult of Mary, but it reached its apogee in 626, during the Avar siege of the city, when the Virgin was believed to have personally participated in the city's defence, and miraculously saved it from the barbarian onslaught. As the hymn of thanks composed by the Patriarch of Constantinople at the time declared,

> Unto you, O Theotokos [*She Who Bore God*], invincible Champion,
> your City, in thanksgiving, ascribes the victory for the deliverance
> from sufferings. And having your might unassailable, free us from
> all dangers, so that we may cry unto you: Rejoice O Bride
> Ever-Virgin!

With the loss of Jerusalem to first the Persians and then the Arabs in the 7th century, Constantinople also began to be imagined as a 'New Jerusalem', home to the remains of the True Cross that had been smuggled out of the Church of the Holy Sepulchre as the Arab armies had advanced (see Chapter 3).

Another reason, however, why Byzantine emperors after Justinian generally chose not to build on a large scale, is that they probably did not need to. The population of Constantinople, as we have seen, is likely to have peaked under Justinian at about 500,000, before the city was struck by the plague. The bubonic plague continued to return periodically to lay low each new generation for approximately the next two hundred years. Only gradually, from the late 8th century, did population levels begin to rise, until they probably reached something approximating their Justinianic levels under the Comnenian emperors of the late 11th and 12th centuries, before collapsing once more as a result of the destruction wrought in the city by the Latin conquest of 1204, and the advent in the 14th century of the Black Death.

We should probably imagine a population oscillating in terms of size between a height of around half a million under Justinian and the Comnenians, and a low of perhaps as few as 40,000–70,000 under the Isaurian emperors of the 8th century and the Palaiologi of the 14th. In the 7th century, as we will see in Chapter 3, the empire also lost control of Egypt, leading to the cutting off of the grain shipments and the abolition of the free distribution of bread. A resultant crisis in the food supply is also likely to have reduced the city's population.

Certainly, there are signs that the Constantinople of the 7th and 8th centuries was not what it had once been: in 626, as noted earlier, the Avars had attempted to cut off the city's water supply by disabling the Aqueduct of Valens; it was not to be repaired until the reign of the Emperor Constantine V (741–75), indicating that reduced supplies were now sufficient for a diminished population. Likewise, whereas in 542 Justinian had been obliged to bury plague victims in mass graves beyond the city walls, or had cast them into the sea, when, in the mid-8th century, the 'Justinianic plague' (as it is known) struck for the last time, Constantine V was able to bury the dead within the walls of the city. The inference must be that there was now plenty of space for them.

Constantine V's decision to bury the dead within the city walls was also a reflection, however, of changing attitudes to the dead. The Greeks and Romans of old had been determined to keep the living away from the dead: the *polis* was the proper abode for the former; the *necropolis* for the latter. Christianity, however, with its veneration of deceased martyrs at their burial sites and attachment to the relics of saints, had gradually broken down the mental barrier that Roman law and Graeco-Roman *mores* had so strenuously sought to uphold.

Likewise, urban life in Constantinople from the 6th to 8th centuries altered and evolved in directions that were partly determined by objective crises (see Chapter 3), but also by broader processes of cultural change. Life in medieval Constantinople became more private and more focused on the household. At the same time, under the influence of the Church, the inhabitants of the city became less at ease with public displays of nudity, or of burlesque. Accordingly, both the amphitheatre and the great baths (such as the Baths of Zeuxippus, also damaged in the Nika riots) fell out of use.

In a striking reinvention of public space, certain of the monumental public squares of the late antique city were reused in the medieval period as markets for livestock, while the Roman amphitheatre by the old *agora* became an execution ground. As will be returned to in Chapter 6, changing attitudes to art, and the loss of many of the artisanal skills of antiquity, also meant that the statues with which Constantine and his heirs had adorned the city were increasingly regarded with a mixture of suspicion and fear, as the abode of demons rather than symbols of high culture.

Likewise, a recasting of the central institutions of the East Roman state in the 7th and 8th centuries would render obsolete the offices of the Praetorian Prefect and other governmental services, with the nuts and bolts of imperial administration increasingly concentrated within the palace. But the essential contours and appearance of the Christian and Roman city as bequeathed by Justinian remained intact.

As indicated earlier, the influence exerted by the Church and Christian institutions on the urban topography of Constantinople was continuous and cumulative: even in the most straitened of circumstances, emperors continued to build and endow churches, monasteries, and charitable foundations in the city. Importantly, members of the court and the aristocracy emulated such imperial philanthropy, founding churches, monasteries, and charitable institutions of their own (from the 7th century, the imperial aristocracy was more palatine or court-focused in nature, and thus more prone to follow and imitate imperial habits).

Setting aside the world of the palace, by the 10th and 11th centuries Constantinople would be dominated by aristocratic households (*oikoi*) on the one hand, many of them still situated in residences first constructed for the late antique aristocracy from the 4th to 6th centuries, and monastic and ecclesiastical institutions founded by imperial and lay benefactors on the other.

Both the aristocratic households and religious institutions derived income from shops and warehouses in the city, as well as extensive estates in the provinces beyond, especially in Thrace, Macedonia, and western Asia Minor. In structural, economic, and even architectural terms, these aristocratic and ecclesiastical *oikoi* were broadly similar (the latter perhaps unsurprising given that many monasteries, such as that of St John of Stoudios between the Constantinian and Theodosian walls, had originated as aristocratic residences or villas). As St Symeon the New Theologian put it at the time (addressing an ecclesiastical audience):

> What is the world and the things of the world? Listen! It is not gold, not silver, nor horses, nor indeed mules; all these things, which minister to the needs of the body, we too acquire. Not bread, not meat, not wine, for we too partake of these and eat sufficiently. Not houses, not baths, not villages or vineyards or estates, for religious institutions (*lavrai*) and monasteries consist of such things too.

Members of the Byzantine aristocracy evidently founded such religious institutions both out of piety and with a view to the afterlife. Such acts of generosity, however, were also advantageous for other reasons. Roman and Byzantine aristocrats had long been interested in trying to ensure the dynastic survival of their families by seeking to prohibit their heirs from giving away or selling their property to non-relatives. Roman and Byzantine law, however, made this very hard to achieve: Justinian, for example, had decreed that such conditions on heirs could only last for three generations. What the law did permit, however, was for aristocratic donors to found monasteries and other religious institutions, endowing them with lucrative investments and estates, on condition that such monasteries guaranteed their descendants (in perpetuity) a fixed share of their revenues.

One reason why founding religious institutions became so popular in Byzantium, therefore, and why the medieval city of Constantinople became so physically and institutionally dominated by monasteries, was because they were the closest thing that Roman and Byzantine law got to 'trust funds'. Donors could look after the posthumous fate of their souls as well as arranging for the future prosperity of their descendants. For both aristocracy and Church, it was a fortuitous combination.

Order and disorder

The medieval city of Constantinople remained commercially vibrant and culturally cosmopolitan. In the 12th century, for example, when population levels were once more returning to something approximating to their Justinianic height, the city was able to provide itself with corn through largely commercial channels.

Likewise, despite the ever closer identification between 'Roman' and 'Christian' identity in the Byzantine imagination, the city remained home to a large Jewish population. By the 10th century there also existed a colony of Muslim Arab merchants, who were permitted their own mosque, while, in the 11th century, as noted earlier, the area around the Golden Horn became home to colonies of Italian merchants (from Venice, Genoa, Pisa, and Amalfi), who would come to play an increasingly important role in the economic life of the empire. Since the 7th and 8th centuries, moreover, many of the highest offices of state had come to be held by men of Armenian and Caucasian origin.

Constantinople continued, therefore, to be the bustling, cacophonous, polyglot centre of power and exchange it had always been. As the Byzantine poet John Tzetzes famously wrote around the middle of the 12th century: 'among Scythians you will find me a Scythian, a Latin among Latins, and among all other nations as if I were one of their race...I address proper and suitable words to everyone, knowing that this is a sign of the best conduct'.

The main changes the city saw around the time that Tzetzes wrote were that the establishment of the Italian trading colonies served to revive a region of the city that had gone into relative economic decline in the 6th century, while, under the Comnenian emperors, the imperial court made less use of the old palace complex by the Hippodrome, and moved to a palace in the Blachernai district to the north-west. This was in much closer proximity to the city walls, and thus allowed emperors greater oversight of the city's defences at a time of mounting military danger.

In Byzantine imperial ideology, emperors were obliged to maintain order (Greek, *taxis*), in emulation of God's benign ordering of the cosmos. Nowhere was this more of a challenge than with respect to the imperial capital itself, where the population seemed always on the brink of getting out of control.

In Justinian's day, as we have seen, the emperor was obliged to contend with mass immigration from the countryside and the violence of the circus factions. His laws also reveal him attempting to regulate the seedier side of city life: cracking down on people traffickers who lured country girls into the great city with promises of shoes and fancy food only to force them into prostitution, or passing laws against homosexuality ('pederasty') and actors, actresses, and prostitutes who chose to dress up as monks, priests, and nuns for the titillation and amusement of their audiences and clients.

It is striking that the only people known to have been punished for homosexual acts under Justinian were bishops, while Procopius records that North African clergy resident in the city were caught consorting with its whores. The city was evidently less 'holy' than official propaganda allowed, and less pious than the wave of monastic foundations might otherwise suggest.

The moral character of the city's populace did not necessarily improve in the post-Justinianic era: a double-sided relief sculpture held by the Archaeological Museum in Istanbul, for example, which has been dated to around the 11th century, appears to depict a priapic bear with a chain round its neck and a naked man wearing a dog mask. For whom, or for what purpose, this sculpture was made must remain a matter of speculation. In almost any context, however, it would seem distinctly odd.

Nor was bad behaviour unknown even at court. The Byzantines (like the ancient Romans before them) enjoyed being entertained, for example, by jesters called *grylloi*, who would cavort suggestively wearing little more than a floppy hat and typically carrying two sticks. In particular, such *grylloi* would expose and wobble their rears to entertain the crowd. According to one (admittedly hostile) source, the dissolute Emperor Michael III (842–67, also known as 'the Drunkard') befriended one such clown and persuaded him to sit next him in the imperial throne room or *Chrysotriklinos* dressed as the Patriarch of Constantinople. When Michael's mother, Theodora, entered the room, she duly knelt before him and asked the supposed patriarch to say a prayer on her behalf. The jester responded to the pious widow's request by turning his rear towards her and emitting what the author describes as 'a donkey-like noise from his foul entrails'.

The urban population also remained prone to rioting: an uprising directed against the Italian colonists in 1182, for example, served to fatally poison relations between the Comnenians and the West. Ensuring plentiful food and supplies remained the key to keeping the population happy and rallying them behind the ruling emperor.

The Patriarch Nicephorus, for example, who despised the 8th-century Emperor Constantine V (741–75) for his opposition to religious images or 'icons', complained that his reign was remembered among the common people as an era of plenty, characterized by cheap food, when in fact it was a time of 'plagues, earthquakes, shooting stars, famines and civil wars'. Yet, he continued, 'these utterly mindless lower animals brag and boast loudly about those "happy days", they say, of abundance'. What could one expect of such people?

> Most of them don't even know the names of the letters of the alphabet and despise and abuse those who set store by education. The roughest and rudest of them are short even of the necessities of life; they couldn't so much as feed themselves for a single day, coming as they do from the crossroads and alley-ways.

Indeed, it is striking that one of the few offices not abolished (or even substantially reformed) amid the reconfiguration of Byzantine administration in the 7th and 8th centuries was that of the Urban Prefect of Constantinople, whose responsibility it was to maintain order in the city. He was also charged with overseeing its food supply and regulating what might be thought of as the 'commanding heights' of the Constantinopolitan economy.

This emerges with particular clarity from a text dating from either the late 9th or early 10th century called the *Book of the Prefect* (*Eparchikon Biblion*), a set of guidelines issued to the Urban Prefect concerning those Constantinopolitan guilds responsible either for the handling or production of food, commercial services, and money, or the supplying of goods needed for ceremonial purposes by the imperial court.

Thus we find regulations relating to bakers, grocers, fishmongers, dealers of either home-produced textiles or textiles imported from the Muslim east, *perfumiers*, dealers in soap and wax, salesmen of incense, pork butchers, lamb and beef butchers, as well as legal notaries, bankers, and money changers. And these were only the trades that were of particular interest to the imperial authorities, over which they were keen to exercise supervision and control. One should imagine a much broader swathe of largely unregulated commercial activity beyond this.

It is also evident that livestock and other commodities (such as timber) were moved vast distances from throughout the empire to reach the market in Constantinople. Even the ceremonial rhythm of the court was calibrated to coincide with the rhythm of the city's food supply. A 10th-century compilation of imperial rituals known as the *Book of Ceremonies* records, amid the processions whereby the emperor and his entourage criss-crossed the city, the protocols to be followed when a formal visitation was paid to the grain silos of the *Strategion*.

When it came to feeding the city, nothing could be left to chance, nor, it would seem, to trust. As the *Book of Ceremonies* records: 'It is also necessary for a surveyor to follow closely behind the emperor, so that if he wants to be satisfied whether so much grain really is stored there, the surveyor can measure whatever places the emperor inspects and tell him the truth'. Only when the emperor was fully reassured could the procession move on.

Chapter 3
From antiquity to the Middle Ages

Containing the crisis

In the late 4th century, the Roman Empire had come to be divided into two parts, each (for the most part) with a separate ruler: the Eastern Empire (comprising Greece, Asia Minor and Anatolia, Syria, Palestine, and Egypt) and the Western Empire (consisting of Italy, Gaul, Britain, the Iberian peninsula, and Africa), with the dividing line between the two parts running through Illyricum in the Balkans.

In the early 5th century, however, the empire as a whole came under sustained military pressure from the Huns and various Germanic peoples from beyond the Rhine and Danube. This pressure was especially pronounced with respect to the empire's western provinces, which bore the brunt of barbarian invasion and were progressively lost to central imperial control, such that, by the early 470s, the Western Empire barely extended beyond Italy.

In 476, the last western Roman emperor, Romulus Augustulus ('the little Augustus') was deposed by the Gothic general Odoacer, who wrote to Constantinople informing the imperial authorities there that there was now longer any need for an emperor in the west.

In place of a unifying trans-Mediterranean Roman hegemony, therefore, by the end of the 5th century autonomous kingdoms had emerged in Italy, Spain, Gaul, and Africa under Gothic, Frankish, Burgundian, and Vandal overlordship. Roman control was even lost in Rome itself.

While the leaders of some of these regimes (such as the Burgundians in Savoy) continued to pay lip service to the concept of overarching imperial suzerainty emanating from the seat of the remaining Roman emperor in Constantinople, others, such as the Vandals, openly defied the imperial court, and pointedly contested the emperor's claims to universal authority, while, at the same time adopting, at their own courts, an increasingly imperial style of rule. In Spain and southern Gaul, for example, the Gothic regime (assisted by Roman courtiers) began to revise and update Roman law with respect to property and other sensitive issues, thereby infringing upon what was deemed to be an imperial prerogative.

To add insult to injury, the Goths and Vandals also publicly rejected what had become the imperially sanctioned definition of the Christian faith. The Christian community in the age of Constantine had been wracked by theological disputes. Accordingly, in 325, at the city of Nicaea, Constantine had convened the first council of the Church as a whole (an 'Ecumenical Council'), both to resolve issues concerned with the governance of the Church and also to settle the main theological dispute, as to whether, within the 'Holy Trinity' of God the Father, God the Son, and God the Holy Spirit, the Father and Son were equal and coexistent through all time. A subsequent council was convened in 381 by Theodosius I to clarify the same issue.

These councils had denounced the teachings of a 4th-century churchman from Alexandria, known as Arius, who had argued for the superiority of God the Father. The barbarians, by contrast, sided with Arius, during whose period of theological ascendancy they had first been evangelized, and whose doctrinal stance allowed them to distance themselves further from Constantinople.

The demise of Roman power in the west and the emergence of the post-Roman successor kingdoms thus constituted a direct challenge to the authority of the remaining Roman emperor in Constantinople, who claimed to be the sole heir to Augustus, with rightful jurisdiction over all territories that had once been Roman. This fact was not lost on political circles in Constantinople in the early 6th century, where the disparity between the emperor's theoretical claims to universal authority and his evident powerlessness over much former Roman territory helped to generate an outpouring of political speculation and debate as to the nature of the imperial office.

At the same time, political tensions in Constantinople in the early 6th century are likely to have been heightened by a number of other threats and issues that loomed on the horizon. In the 5th century, largely peaceful relations had been established between the East Roman Empire and Persia. The rulers of both these empires had felt themselves to be threatened by the Huns, and accordingly they had cooperated against the barbarians in their midst. It was probably the negotiation of this peace with Persia that had enabled the East Roman Empire to surmount the crisis of the 5th century.

The early 6th century, however, had seen the revival of warfare between the empires. In 502, the Persians had launched what was perceived from Constantinople to be an entirely unprovoked assault on Roman Syria. While the Persians had eventually been persuaded to withdraw their forces in return for the payment of tribute, warfare had been costly and can only have served to excite a deep sense of insecurity on the part of many of the inhabitants of the empire's eastern provinces and those who owned land there, including high-ranking members of the senate in Constantinople. Through this senatorial connection, perceived military weakness on the fringes of Syria had a profound impact on political conditions in the imperial capital.

The revival of warfare with Persia also carried with it other, more far-reaching implications. For it meant that emperors had no choice but to upgrade the empire's military capacity and defensive infrastructure. Each of these required money, and money meant taxation (it has been estimated, for example, that the Roman army received somewhere in the region of one-half to two-thirds of all tax revenues collected by the Roman state).

Yet effective taxation was something that, since the mid-4th century, Roman emperors had found it increasingly difficult to achieve. As seen in Chapter 1, the 4th century had witnessed the emergence across the Roman world of a new imperial aristocracy of service, whose members had come to dominate both the highest offices of the state and also, increasingly, local landed society. Although their highly productive estates helped fuel economic growth, from a fiscal perspective, this would prove to be a highly ominous development.

Late Roman taxation was primarily levied on the land and those who worked it, and the ascendancy of the new aristocracy of service meant that a growing share of the land was passing into the ownership of individuals who, by virtue of the governmental positions and connections that they enjoyed, were especially well placed to evade the taxes to which their estates were liable (and which they were often charged with collecting).

From the late 4th century, tax evasion on the part of such landowners can be seen to have become a growing cause for concern on the part of emperors, who also expressed mounting anxiety at the willingness and ability of such landowners to flout other aspects of imperial law by, for example, suborning imperial troops to serve as private armed retainers on their estates, or illicitly building prisons on their properties with which to intimidate and cajole their workforce. The revival of warfare with

Persia in the early 6th century served to increase the pressure on the imperial government to address this situation by seeking to strengthen the writ of the emperor and his law in the provinces.

The undermining of imperial authority was intensified by one further development. The Council of Constantinople in 381 had effectively closed down debate within the imperial Church with respect to Trinitarian theology. As a result, theologians and churchmen began to debate the relationship between the human and divine in the person of Jesus Christ, who was meant to be both fully human and fully divine. This debate over 'Christology' had become increasingly heated as a result of the claim of an early 5th-century Patriarch of Constantinople by the name of Nestorius, who had denied that the Virgin Mary (who was emerging as the city's patron) should be called the 'Theotokos' ('She who Bore God') as she could only have given birth to the human Jesus.

Nestorius had been deposed, but his opponents in the Church in Syria, Egypt, and elsewhere (led by Cyril, Patriarch of Alexandria) felt that the Christological definition established at the resultant Church Council at Chalcedon in 451 had given too much ground to those who were determined to draw sharp distinctions between Christ's human and divine natures, and accordingly they had rejected it. The decrees of such ecumenical councils, however, carried the status of imperial law. To gainsay them was thus not only to resist the will of God but also the will of the emperor.

Each of these challenges to imperial authority elicited a determined response during the early years of the reign of the Emperor Justinian, whose period in office would prove to be a watershed in the evolution of the Byzantine world. The reforms initiated by Justinian in the period from *c.* 527–44 must be viewed as a whole. Like the dome of his great monument in Constantinople, the Church of Holy Wisdom, or Hagia Sophia, the overarching concept of the reassertion of imperial dignity was dependent upon the supporting substructures of a disorientatingly diverse range of policies encompassing religion, the law, provincial administration, fiscal policy, and imperial ideology.

Justinian's first priority was to reassert imperial control over the religious lives of his subjects. Among the first acts of the new emperor in the years 528–9, were measures instituting the concerted persecution of surviving pagans among the upper classes, as well as heretics and homosexuals. Likewise, the year 532 saw the first of Justinian's repeated efforts to reconcile the pro- and anti-Chalcedonian elements within the Church. This attempt combined an apparently genuine effort to establish a theological position with which all could concur, with a ruthless determination to punish and exclude those individual bishops who had led resistance to the imperial authorities.

At the same time, the emperor sought to provide an ideological justification for the active part he was determined to play in the religious life of his subjects. More explicitly than any emperor before him, Justinian asserted that the authority of the emperor and that of the priesthood derived from a common divine source. Imperial ceremonial adopted an increasingly religious tone, emphasizing the unique place of the emperor at the intersection of the divine and earthly hierarchies of power.

This determined effort to reposition the emperor at the heart of the religious life of his subjects proceeded alongside an attempt to reassert imperial control over the secular structures of government. Between 528 and 534 Justinian's advisers reformed and codified the civil law of the empire. The inherited legal framework was remodelled to serve contemporary needs, and the emperor was established, for the first time in Roman tradition, as the one and only legitimate source of law. The person of the emperor was, Justinian decreed, 'the law animate'.

As the new legal framework of the empire took shape, so too, in 535, did Justinian attempt to render recourse to the law on the part of his subjects more practicable. Between 535 and 539, Justinian legislated on the administrative and governmental structures of no fewer than seventeen provinces, in an attempt to make governors less prone to the corrupting blandishments offered by the patronage of aristocratic landowners and to secure the collection of vital tax revenues. As Justinian declared in 539 in his edict on Egypt, tax evasion on the part of city councillors, landowners, and imperial officials threatened 'the very cohesion of our state itself'.

Such a concerted series of reforms was bound to elicit internal opposition, not least on the part of those aristocratic interests to whom active imperial rule was by no means a necessarily attractive option. The first and most dramatic expression of discontent erupted in the year 532 with the Nika riots (see Chapter 2), which the emperor crushed amid the horrific bloodbath in the city's Hippodrome.

At the same time Justinian took an aggressive stance towards the empire's rivals to the east, north, and west. Justinian invested heavily in the empire's defensive infrastructure along its Persian frontier and in the Balkans, and sought to extend the empire's influence among the peoples of the Caucasus and Arabia, using missionary activity and conversion as well as subsidies and force of arms to draw them into an increasingly Constantinopolitan orbit.

Militarily, the eastern and northern frontiers were Justinian's chief concerns. Nevertheless, in the 530s the emperor took advantage of political instability in the Vandal kingdom of North Africa and the Ostrogothic regime in Italy to attempt to restore direct Roman rule over these territories. In many respects, a bit like the reconstruction of Hagia Sophia, these were campaigns on the cheap: only some 15,000 or so men were sent to North Africa, and it is unlikely that there were ever more than 30,000 troops engaged in active service during the long drawn-out Italian campaign.

These western forays were, nevertheless, successful. North Africa fell in 533–4, and Italy was conquered between 535 and 553. In the early 550s, Justinian's armies were even able to establish a foothold in southern Spain. These victories did much to restore the empire to a position of political, ideological, and military dominance in the central and western Mediterranean (Map 3).

From the beginning of the 540s, however, the mood of ambition and confidence that had characterized the first fourteen years of Justinian's reign began to give way to a rather more sombre attitude. There appear to have been a number of reasons for this. First, in spite of Justinian's aggressive stance towards Persia, the Sasanians were still capable of breaching the empire's eastern defences. In 540, the Persian Shah Khusro I was able to obviate Roman defences in Mesopotamia and sack the city of Antioch, an event which left a deep impression on the contemporary Procopius, who wrote that he 'became dizzy' when he attempted to report the calamity.

Second, from the late 550s the imperial position in the Balkans was undermined by the arrival to the north of the Danube of a powerful nomadic group fleeing political and military instability on the Eurasian Steppe. Forced westwards by the expansion to the north of the Caucasus and the Black Sea of the Western Turk Empire, a people known as the Avars came to establish themselves in the Danubian basin. Although Justinian was initially able to incorporate the Avars into his tribal policy, their arrival was ominous.

Perhaps more crucially, Justinian's internal, fiscal, and religious policies themselves began to falter. It was becoming increasingly evident that the dispute over Chalcedon was an essentially insoluble one. In 553, at the Second Council of Constantinople, Justinian's theologians did in fact piece together a formula that ought to have addressed the concerns of all parties concerned. By this stage, however, the tradition of conflict over Chalcedon was so

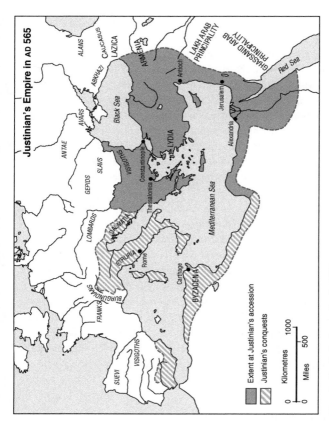

Map 3. Justinian's empire in 565.

49

ingrained in the minds of the participants that few were interested in restoring peace to the Church.

But above all, in the 540s, as we have seen in Chapter 2, the empire was dealt a body blow with the advent of the bubonic plague, which, originating in central Africa, reached the empire for the first time via the Red Sea in the year 541. From Egypt, the plague soon spread to Constantinople, Palestine, Syria, Asia Minor, the Balkans, North Africa, and Italy. Both the cities of the empire and their rural hinterlands were severely affected by the initial impact of the disease and its subsequent recurrences. The population of the empire may have been reduced by a third. Not only did this mean much human misery, it also dramatically reduced the number of taxpayers on whom the state could rely. This in turn led to administrative paralysis, and a number of Justinian's provincial reforms had to be reversed.

In 565 Justinian died. As the court poet Corippus put it: 'the awesome death of the man showed by clear signs that he had conquered the world. He alone, amid universal lamentations, seemed to rejoice in his pious countenance'. The memory of Justinian (Figure 4) was to loom large in the minds of subsequent generations of emperors, just as the physical monuments built in Constantinople during his reign were long to dominate the medieval city. Nevertheless, in spite of the grandeur of Justinian's project, a reign that had promised much ultimately ended in disappointment. Justinian bequeathed to his successor, Justin II (565–74), an empire which, though larger, was, nevertheless, markedly fragile and fiscally unstable.

Heraclius and holy war

This fiscal instability in particular was to do much to undermine the reigns of Justinian's successors and limit their ability to meet increasingly pressing military needs. Justin II declared upon his accession that he 'found the treasury burdened with many debts

4. Mosaic panel from San Vitale, Ravenna, depicting the Emperor Justinian (6th century).

and reduced to utter exhaustion'. The emperor was consequently unwilling, or unable, to continue the subventions by which the empire had secured the support of its allies in northern Arabia, as well as, more recently, the Avars in the Balkans.

The consolidation of Avar power to the north of the Danube rendered Justinian's policy of 'divide and rule' less and less effective. Both Slavs and Lombards attempted to flee Avar domination, entering into imperial territory in the Balkans and Italy respectively. Between 568 and 572 much of northern Italy fell to the Lombards. In the 580s, a number of cities in the Balkans from Thessalonica to Athens suffered repeated Avar and Slav attacks, the Avars concentrating on the plains to the north, the Slavs taking advantage of mountainous highlands and forest cover to strike and settle ever further south. As military pressures mounted, financial crisis deepened. In 588, military pay was reduced by 25 per cent, leading to a major mutiny on the empire's eastern frontier.

In the year 602, imperial forces were campaigning against Slav tribes beyond the Danube. The reigning Emperor Maurice (581–602) ordered that the troops continue the campaign into the winter. The emperor was already unpopular within military circles due to his economizing, and the Danubian army erupted into open revolt under the leadership of an officer by the name of Phocas. The army marched on Constantinople, slaughtered Maurice and his family, and elevated Phocas to the imperial throne, in the first successful *coup d'état* since the accession of Constantine.

The fall of Maurice and the accession of Phocas (602–10) saw the empire's descent into a protracted civil war. The Persian Shah Khusro II seized upon this opportunity to strike deep into Roman positions in the Caucasus and Syria. By 610 the Persians had reached the Euphrates, while by 611 they were advancing into Anatolia. These dramatic Persian victories catalysed and were facilitated by further political instability. In particular, in 610 the son of the governor of Africa, Heraclius, arrived outside the imperial capital at the head of a fleet, intent on overthrowing Phocas. The emperor's supporters rapidly deserted him and Heraclius (610–41) thereupon was crowned.

The Persians took advantage of Roman disarray to complete the conquest of Syria and Palestine. In 613 Damascus fell, while in 614 a victorious Persian army entered Jerusalem, where, amid much general slaughter, the remains of the True Cross were seized and sent off to Persia. By 615, a cowed Constantinopolitan senate was willing to sue for peace. A high-ranking embassy was dispatched to Khusro II. The Shah was addressed as 'supreme emperor', and Heraclius was described as the Shah's 'true son, eager to perform the services of your serenity in all things'. The senate was willing to acknowledge the Persian Empire as superior to that of Rome, and the Roman emperor as the Shah's client. Khusro's response was forthright. The ambassadors were executed. No mercy was to be shown. Persia was determined to eliminate its ancient imperial rival.

The Persians were now ready to initiate the conquest of Egypt. In 619, Alexandria fell, and within the year the entire province would appear to have been in Persian hands. All that now remained was for the Persians to resume the advance into Anatolia and make their way to Constantinople. The Persians were now applying inexorable pressure on what remained of the empire. Heraclius was faced with a stark choice: he could either wait for the Persian grip to tighten, fighting a series of rearguard actions which offered little chance of ultimate success, or he could throw caution to the wind and take battle to the enemy. Heraclius opted for the latter.

Between 615 and 622 the emperor had instituted a series of crisis measures aimed at maximizing the resources at his disposal. Official salaries and military pay had been halved and governmental structures overhauled. Churches were stripped of their gold ornaments and silver plate and the wealth of the cities was drained. These funds were used to attempt to buy peace with the Avars in the west, and to elicit the support of the Christian population of the Transcaucasus and the occupied territories. This effort was reinforced by a religious propaganda drive, emphasizing the horrors associated with the fall of Jerusalem, and playing upon the apocalyptic sensibilities that were a pronounced feature of the day. At the same time, the emperor set about organizing an intensively trained infantry force versed in the tactics of guerrilla warfare and enthused with religious fervour. A concept of Christian 'holy war' against the Persian infidel came to be enunciated.

There was little point in Heraclius attempting to engage the superior Persian forces on open terrain. Rather, the emperor realized that his best hope would be to head north, to the highlands of the Caucasus, where he would be able to request reinforcements from the Christian principalities of the region, and where a small, highly mobile army might yet outwit a numerically preponderant foe.

In 624 Heraclius departed from Constantinople. Advancing up the Euphrates, the Romans marched into Persian Armenia, laying waste to a number of cities as they went, and destroying the premier fire-temple of the Zoroastrian religion of the shah*s* at Takht-i-Suleiman as explicit vengeance for the massacring of the Christians of Jerusalem. Soon thereafter Heraclius issued his summons to the Christian lords of the region, while also sending an embassy to the Turks to the north of the Caucasus, in an attempt to negotiate an alliance with the formidable steppe power.

Repeated attempts by the Persians to pin down and trap Heraclius in the mountains and valleys of the Caucasus failed. Accordingly, in 626 the Persians attempted to draw him out by launching a joint attack with the Avars on Constantinople. As seen in Chapter 2, however, the Avar siege failed (supposedly thwarted by the personal intervention of the Virgin Mary). Heraclius, moreover, had failed to take the bait, and had continued to nurture his Caucasian alliances.

It was now that the emperor activated the alliance with the Turks. In 627, a joint Roman and Turk army stormed Persia's northern defences between the Caucasus and the Caspian and pressed south to the Zagros mountains in the heart of Persia. The Turks then returned north, but Heraclius pressed on until he was able to bear down upon the Persian capital at Ctesiphon, reducing the wealthy estates and towns around it to ash and rubble in emulation of the 'scorched earth' tactics that Khusro II's armies had adopted in Asia Minor.

Among military and court circles in Ctesiphon panic set in, and on 24 March 628 notice reached Heraclius that Khusro II had been deposed in a coup and was dead. The negotiations that ensued restored the True Cross to Jerusalem and Roman control to the Near East. As the victory dispatch to Constantinople announced: 'fallen is the arrogant Khusro, the enemy of God. He is fallen and cast down to the depths of the earth, and his memory is utterly exterminated.'

Restoration and collapse

The Eastern Empire was thus restored, or at least it was to some extent. The imperial concentration on the east, for example, had led to a further dramatic weakening of its position in the Balkans. Although the Avar confederacy lay in ruins in the aftermath of the defeat of 626, not only the highlands, but increasingly the lowlands of the Balkans were coming to be settled by autonomous Slav tribes.

The cities of Anatolia and Asia Minor had been exhausted by the financial exertions of warfare. Many of them stood in ruin as a result of Persian attack. In Syria, Palestine, and Egypt, the reassertion of imperial control at this point must have been largely nominal. Long-standing traditions of government had been dislocated and were yet to be restored. However, before any such restoration could take place, the empire found itself faced with a new challenge from its extended and largely undefended Arabian frontier.

The rivalry between Rome and Persia of the 6th and early 7th centuries had involved both empires in a series of military and diplomatic dealings with the Arab tribes to their south. This involvement within the region on the part of the great powers would appear to have sparked off what some historians have characterized as a 'nativist revolt' among elements within Arabian society, whereby they united against foreign interference, while appropriating certain of the creeds and ideas that had been brought into Arabia from the outside, and in the process forging an autonomous religious and political identity.

The Arabs had been told, for example, by Christian missionaries and Jews that they were descended from Ishmael, first-born son of the Biblical Prophet Abraham, whom Abraham had cast out into the desert. Likewise, they had learned from the same sources that the world was in its last days, and divine judgement was imminent. These, and other more heterodox ideas, swirled around in a syncretist milieu that proved to be fertile ground for the emergence or acceptance of new systems of belief, and new forms of political affiliation.

In particular, in the 620s the tribes of Arabia had come to be united under the leadership of a religious leader originating from Mecca known as Muhammad ('the blessed one'). Muhammad preached a rigorously monotheist doctrine, strongly influenced by apocalyptic trends within contemporary Christianity, and by Messianic fervour among the Jews of the region.

Divine judgement, he preached, was indeed imminent, and all were to submit themselves to the will of the one God. In particular, all Arabs were to set aside their inherited religious traditions and political rivalries and embrace the new faith. In return, Muhammad declared, as descendants of Abraham's first-born son, Ishmael, God would grant the Arabs mastery over the Holy Land that He had promised to Abraham and his seed forever. Perhaps influenced by propaganda disseminated during the course of Heraclius' struggle against Khusro II, this return to the Holy Land was to be achieved by means of holy war.

Muhammad is said to have died around the year 632, but his creed lived on, and the community of believers that he established (known as the *Umma*) rapidly filled the power vacuum in northern Arabia, southern Syria, and southern Iraq created by the exhaustion of the two great powers and the consequent collapse of their clientage networks among the Arab tribes.

From 633/4, Roman Palestine suffered savage Arab incursions that combined the massacring of the rural population with assaults on towns and cities. Although the size of the Arab armies would seem to have been relatively small, the imperial authorities were evidently in little position to offer effective resistance. Intelligence as to the nature of the Arab threat appears to have been limited, while the rapid advance of the Arab line of battle gave the imperial forces little time to regroup.

Faced with such a situation, a number of cities in the Transjordan, Palestine, and Syria simply capitulated: Jerusalem was probably taken by the end of 635 (though many sources give a later date), while in 636 a large Roman army was decisively defeated near the Yarmuk River in northern Jordan. Thereafter, conquest was swift, as retreating Roman forces were pursued into Egypt. The weakness of the Roman response led the invaders to campaign ever further afield, such that the Persians too soon felt the brunt of Arab assaults, and by 656 their empire was no more.

Only as they found themselves forced back into Anatolia and Asia Minor were the East Roman commanders able to begin to stem the enemy advance. The civil strife of the early 7th century and the years of warfare with Persia had clearly inflicted lasting damage.

When, in 641, Heraclius died, the empire was collapsing around him once more. The eastern Roman Empire of Byzantium now faced its second great struggle for survival, one which was to dominate its early medieval history.

The end of the ancient world

Islam as a religion and the Arabs as a people were themselves the products of late antiquity, and, in particular, of the political and religious conditions that had come to prevail in northern Arabia by virtue of mounting East Roman and Persian rivalry. At the same time however, the Arab conquests of the early 7th century effectively destroyed the ancient world by sweeping away the political polarity of Rome and Persia on which it had come to rest.

The East Roman Empire in the 640s was in a state of political, military, and demographic collapse (the latter by virtue of repeated bouts of the bubonic plague), and was too exhausted for the emperors Constans II (641–68) and Justinian II (685–95 and 705–11) to roll back the enemy tide even when two outbreaks of blood-letting and civil war within the nascent Islamic empire appeared to present the opportunity. Unlike the Persian Empire, however, Byzantium survived, and it did so largely through a remarkable assertion of statecraft.

The reigns of Justinian and Heraclius had already revealed evidence for considerable political and cultural creativity in the East Roman state. Justinian's programme of legal reform and interventions in the development and formation of Church doctrine, for example, had effectively recast the imperial office and broken down the remaining barriers between civil society and the realm of belief. His was, to all intents and purposes, a confessional state, in which religious and political identity were fused. Heraclius' 'holy war' rhetoric had elevated this development to a higher level of imaginative reality.

It is under Heraclius, for example, and in propaganda produced on behalf of his court, that we first encounter the concept of the city of Constantinople as a New Jerusalem, and of the empire's pious citizens constituting a New Israel. The emperor declared himself in Greek to be *basileus*, the term used in the Greek Bible to describe the kings of the Old Testament. At the same time, Heraclius' reign had witnessed remarkable creativity and daring in military and strategic thinking, with the adoption of guerrilla tactics against the Persians, and the outlining of a 'grand strategy' for imperial survival through alliance with the dominant nomad power on the West Eurasian Steppe.

In the reign of Heraclius' successors in the 7th and 8th centuries, this creativity would become even more pronounced, and the emergent tendencies of the earlier era would come to be set in stone. The concept of the Byzantines as a New Israel was at the forefront, for example, of propaganda disseminated by the Emperor Justinian II, in whose reign the fusion between Roman and Christian identities was forcefully expressed by his decision to mint gold coins bearing a foreboding image of Christ 'King of Kings' (Figure 5).

In particular, the emperors of the period oversaw the root and branch reform of the empire's administrative system: the late Roman offices of state, such as the Praetorian Prefecture of the East, on which the empire had depended, were simply swept away, as was the regimental structure of the old Roman army and its system of provisioning and supply. Instead, the army was divided into new units called 'themes' (*themata*), the rank-and-file within which were eventually rewarded partly with a cash wage, and partly with a military landholding (*stratiotikon ktema*) which the soldier's family could farm and which he could pass on to his heirs in return for military service. Emperors thus harnessed the economic interests of an emergent soldier peasantry to secure the survival of the state.

The old units of provincial administration were abolished, and instead the empire was divided into new territorial divisions

5. Gold coin of the Emperor Justinian II depicting Christ 'King of Kings' (late 7th century).

initially called *strategiai*, each allocated to the defence of a specific 'thematic' army. Eventually, these new territorial units likewise came to be known as 'themes', within which all civil and military responsibility was entrusted to the commander or *strategos*. The militarization of the Byzantine administration was associated with the fortification of cities from which the *strategoi* governed, which came increasingly to be known as military camps or *kastra*.

The person of the *strategos* was directly answerable to the emperor and his court, and received regular inspections from imperial agents styled *logothetai*, who were the emperor's eyes and ears in the provinces. As a result, the core territories of the Byzantine Empire of the late 7th and 8th centuries were probably the most tightly administered regions anywhere to the west of China (Map 4).

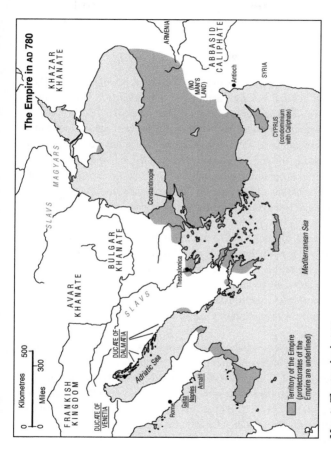

Map 4. The empire in 780.

This assertion of Byzantine statecraft was also partly the result of social processes. Provincial society in the age of Justinian, as we have seen, had been dominated by members of the essentially Constantinian aristocracy of service. The fortunes and properties of many members of this elite, however, had been destroyed amid the warfare of the 7th century. As a result, their power was now at best vestigial.

At a local level, this meant taxes could now be collected and the emperor's will enforced without any consideration given to the interests and concerns of the grand families of old. This was important, for while much of the empire lay in ruins as a result of Persian and later Arab attacks, around Constantinople, in Bithynia and along the coastline of western Asia Minor local economies survived at something approximating their late antique levels of sophistication and prosperity. Such regions were ripe for taxation, and such taxes could fund Byzantine resistance to the Arabs.

Likewise, although in 713 the Emperor Philippikos Bardanes (711–13) is reported to have dined with senators of ancient lineages, at the imperial court the influence of such families had been increasingly supplanted or assimilated by that of a new generation of functionaries, as well as by military hardmen typically of Armenian or Caucasian origin.

As a result, a new palatine or court-focused elite took shape, more economically dependent on the state, and perhaps more ideologically committed to it. Certainly, from the perspective of the emperor, such men were more biddable than the senatorial aristocracy of old. The Byzantine Empire thus emerged from its 7th-century crisis considerably smaller, but with the power of the emperor significantly enhanced.

Chapter 4
Byzantium and Islam

Defining the enemy

By the end of the 7th century, it was evident to the Byzantine authorities that the Arab conquests were no 'flash in the pan' and were not simply going to be rolled back through the creation of a Heraclian style 'grand alliance'. Rather, a new superpower rival had replaced Persia, and was applying constant pressure on what remained of the East Roman Empire in Anatolia and Asia Minor, launching yearly raids from the Arabs' main military bases in Syria.

Indeed, in 654 and 717 the Arabs even managed to lay siege to Constantinople itself, while in 674 an attempt to land armies on the coastline of Asia Minor was only repelled with the aid of the empire's new secret weapon of 'Greek fire', which had been introduced to the Byzantine high command by a Christian refugee from Syria.

But how were the Byzantines to make sense of their new opponent? During the initial phases of the Arab conquests of the 7th century, the armies of the *Umma* appear to have comprised not only Arab tribesmen who had been called to monotheism through the preaching of Muhammad, but also a certain number of Arab Christians and north Arabian Jews. This made the religious character of the armies difficult for outsiders to categorize or identify. This situation was exacerbated by the fact that Islam itself was, at this point, a relatively inchoate movement, not yet fully defined against what are now sometimes termed the other 'Abrahamic' religions of Christianity and Judaism.

Accordingly, some contemporary observers assumed the Muslims essentially to be Jews (not an illogical assumption given that they claimed to worship the God of the Old Testament in accordance with Mosaic law, while also denying the divinity of Christ). Others, such as the 8th-century Orthodox theologian and monk John of Damascus, regarded Islam to have originated as a Christian heresy. Again, such a position was perfectly understandable, given that the Muslim *Qur'an* can be seen to adopt a stance with respect to a range of issues, such as the divinity of Christ and the Crucifixion (both of which it denies, while at the same time according great respect to the figure of Mary and acknowledging the Virgin Birth), which are paralleled in contemporary forms of heterodox and Gnostic Christian thought. From a Byzantine perspective, Islam appeared derivative.

From an early date, Byzantine observers and critics of Islam also identified Muhammad's preaching with respect to religious justifications for violence as a key characteristic of the movement. This was perhaps ironic, given that the Islamic doctrine of *jihad* was taking shape at around the same time as the Emperor Heraclius was advocating a concept of holy war against the infidel Persians, and promising direct entry to paradise to those who died in defence of the faith. But to the end of the Middle Ages, Byzantine perceptions of Islam remained essentially the same: that there was little that was novel or original to the teachings of Muhammad save for the ferocity of the violence that he espoused. As the Byzantine Emperor Manuel II Palaiologos (1391–1425) put it: 'Show me just what Muhammad brought that was new, and there you will find things only cruel and inhuman, such as his command to spread by the sword the faith that he preached.'

With the stabilization and consolidation of Muslim rule over the Near and Middle East, however, the contours of the new religion began to become more clearly defined. A crucial role in this process was played by the caliphs of the Umayyad dynasty who ruled over the Islamic empire as a whole from the late 7th to the middle of the 8th century. From their court at Damascus, the Umayyads both personally directed the *jihad* against Constantinople, and presided over formal disputations between Christian, Jewish, and Muslim scholars that helped to give greater definition to the faith. They also gave greater public visibility to their religion by building magnificent monuments such as the Great Mosque in Damascus and the Dome of the Rock in Jerusalem, and by placing the name and, it would appear, possibly even image of Muhammad on their own gold coinage, which was meant to replace the actual or mock Byzantine coinage in circulation in the former Roman territories over which they ruled.

In response to this reform of the currency, the Emperor Justinian II, as noted in Chapter 3, began to mint gold coins bearing the image of Christ King of Kings. At Damascus, the reigning Caliph Abd al-Malik hit back by drawing upon earlier Jewish critiques of Christian practice to denounce the Christian veneration of religious images (and the emperor's new coinage) as idolatrous and in breach of the Second Commandment against 'graven images'. In doing so, the caliph had for the first time established opposition to religious images as a cornerstone of the Islamic faith, and it is striking that henceforth all coins issued by the caliphate were entirely non-figurative in design.

Rivalry and emulation

The dispute over religious images that became a feature of Byzantine–Islamic rivalry at the end of the 7th century is instructive as it epitomizes the extent to which, from that point onwards, the struggle for mastery of the Near East was increasingly fought on an ideological plane and in competition over a shared symbolic universe framed by the Old Testament, with reference to which both Byzantine emperors and Islamic caliphs sought to justify themselves.

At the same time, the new Arab rulers appropriated and laid claim to elements of the Roman ideological and architectural inheritance. The Dome of the Rock in Jerusalem, for example, is highly reminiscent of contemporary Byzantine ecclesiastical architecture, while the Great Mosque in Damascus is built according to Roman architectural principles and was decorated with exquisite examples of mosaics made from materials sent from Constantinople by way of diplomatic gift. Furthermore, by claiming to be God's Deputy (*khalifat Allah*), Abd al-Malik and his heirs were essentially appropriating the claim that Roman and Byzantine emperors had long been making with respect to the nature of their own authority.

Emulation, however, was a two-way street. From the 690s, as we have seen, the caliphal authorities in Damascus had denounced the Christian veneration of images or 'icons' (Greek *eikones*) of Christ, Mary, and the Saints as idolatrous and in breach of the Second Commandment. There are some indications that the Caliph Yazid II (720–4) may have taken this policy further by ordering the destruction of such images within Christian places of worship under Muslim rule and the whitewashing of churches. Significantly, the early 8th century was also a period of mounting military and political crisis in Byzantium, which many interpreted as evidence that the empire had lost divine favour, and although an Arab siege of Constantinople had been driven back in 717–18, this sense of foreboding was intensified in 726 when a devastating volcanic eruption occurred on the island of Thera.

This loss of divine favour had to be explained. Earlier generations of Byzantines would have accounted for it in terms of Christological heresy, but the Christological teachings of the imperial Church at this point were those that had been established by the Emperor Justinian in the 6th century. From the perspective of the 8th century, Justinian was a manifestly successful ruler whose orthodoxy could not be impugned. Moreover, most of those who had opposed the official definition of the faith now lived in a state of captivity under Muslim rule in Syria and Egypt—hardly a sign of divine approval. Rather, some in court, ecclesiastical, and military circles seemingly decided that perhaps the Muslims had a point, and that the cause of divine displeasure was the Christian veneration of icons.

This sentiment appeared to be confirmed in 727, when a rampaging Arab army failed to take the city of Nicaea, where Constantine the Great had convened the first Ecumenical Council in 325. It was reported that during the course of the siege, a Byzantine soldier (also named Constantine) had thrown a stone at and trampled on an image of the Virgin. Accordingly, some credited the survival of the city to Constantine's intervention (which we know of only through a later, garbled, and hostile account).

Soon thereafter, the Emperor Leo III (717–41) issued an edict declaring that 'the making of icons is a craft of idolatry: they must not be worshiped'. Interestingly, Leo (who had already attempted to regain divine favour by forcibly baptizing Jews) would be denounced by his critics as 'the Saracen-minded'. The official line was then hardened considerably by Leo's son and successor Constantine V (741–75), known in later hostile sources as 'Copronymous' ('shit-named'), who in 754 convened a Church Council at Hieria to put theological flesh on the bones of Leo III's edict. He thereby initiated a struggle over the place of images within the Byzantine Church known as 'iconoclasm' or 'iconomachy'.

Those engaged in this struggle did not have a lot of theological material with which to work. From what we can ascertain, images had played a role in Christian worship since the very earliest days of the Church. They are attested, for example, in the early Christian churches excavated in Dura Europos in Syria, as well as in the catacombs of Rome. From the 6th century, however, religious images had come to play a growing role in the public religion of the empire, and icons were paraded through the streets in imperial ceremonials, or carried into battle in the hope of eliciting divine support.

But at the level of 'popular religion', the veneration of images was already an established fact, and significantly the early use of such images had attracted almost nothing by way of hostile comment on the part of Christian authors at the time, least of all those writing in Greek. They clearly were not regarded as a problem. As a result, neither the anti-icon (or 'iconoclast') party, nor the pro-icon (or 'iconodule') faction had much pre-existing theological literature to fall back on. The iconoclasts thus had to rely at the end of the day on the Second Commandment, while the iconodules essentially had to fall back on the existing traditions of the Church.

What arguably gave iconoclasm political traction was that those emperors most strongly associated with it (Leo III, but especially Constantine V) proved to be highly effective militarily, leading to a particularly strong attachment to iconoclasm on the part of the military rank-and-file. In 787, for example, an attempt to convene a Council to revoke iconoclasm initially had to be abandoned when the meeting was broken up by soldiers loyal to both the memory and theology of Constantine V.

Only as the correlation between military victory and iconoclast theology began to break down over the course of the late 8th and early 9th centuries could the veneration of images be officially rehabilitated, leading in 843 to the so-called 'Triumph of Orthodoxy' whereby iconoclast policy was formally and finally rescinded. Although the scale and extent of the actual destruction of images in this period can be exaggerated, debate over their place in worship would leave a deep imprint on the Byzantine religious and artistic tradition (to which we shall return in Chapter 6).

It should be remembered, however, that the debate had originally been generated by tensions resulting from Byzantium's interaction with Islam. As the phenomenon of iconoclasm reveals, the development and evolution of Byzantium across the 8th, 9th, and 10th centuries was driven above all by the pressing need to contain and respond to the Islamic foe.

A frontier society

For much of this period, the nature of the warfare fought by the Byzantines against the Arabs was rearguard and defensive. Once the Arabs had established effective suzerainty over the lands of the Caucasus by the late 7th century, there was little the Byzantines could do to prevent large-scale incursions. Via their control of Armenia in particular, the Arabs established mastery of the vital east–west passes that gave them open access to the Anatolian plateau. The Byzantines were effectively obliged to fall back on techniques of guerrilla warfare that had first been honed by Heraclius against the Persians.

The eastern frontier between Byzantium and Islam was dominated by mountains. With the exception of the soft, lowland underbelly of Asia Minor, often taken advantage of by the Arab raiders of Tarsus, the undulating plains of Anatolia and the prosperous Arab-held cities which followed the course of the Euphrates were separated by a vast range of mountains, extending from the volcanic highlands of Armenia southwards. Stretches of this mountainous terrain stood more than 4,000 metres above sea level, while the bulk of the range loomed at between 150 and 2,000 metres.

Controlling access across these mountains was thus the first military priority. This could be secured, the Byzantines realized, by relatively small numbers of troops, and mountain passes termed *kleisourai* were fortified to ambush an invading foe, although the Byzantines eventually realized that it was easier to strike at the Arabs as they attempted to return back to the caliphate from imperial territory laden with booty and encumbered by captives than it was to attempt to contain them in the early phases of an attack.

On either side of the mountains lay the plains. These were arid and dusty in the summer and bitterly cold in winter, meaning that the campaigning season was essentially limited to the spring. The relatively narrow campaigning season meant that the Arab armies tended to consist primarily of light cavalry, which the Byzantines attempted to contain with largely locally raised infantry units of the thematic armies. During periods of Arab invasion the civilian population was evacuated to mountain strongholds as well as vast subterranean citadels. Thus the treatise 'On Skirmishing Warfare' attributed to the Emperor Nicephorus II Phocas (963–9) advises that one should 'Evacuate the area well and find refuge for the inhabitants and their flocks on high and rugged mountains.' Likewise, the 10th-century Arab poet Muttanabi describes Byzantine civilians 'Hidden in the rocks and their caves, like serpents in the heart of the earth.'

The scale of the Arab attacks could be massive. In the 8th and 9th centuries, caliphs such as Harun al-Rashid, who could draw upon the resources of the entire Muslim world, would enter Byzantine territory with up to 100,000 men. The Byzantines at this time might have had about that many troops in total in the entirety of their empire. For the Byzantines in this period, to be able to summon 20,000 soldiers for the purpose of a single campaign was pretty exceptional. Direct confrontation with this united Islamic world thus could be of little avail. Rather, the empire was obliged to fight a long drawn-out war of attrition until the Islamic world itself began to fragment.

The world of the frontier was not, however, a closed one penetrated only by marauding armies during the campaigning season. Even during the 7th and 8th centuries, a considerable amount of trade is likely to have crossed the frontier. Certainly, exchange on a high level, regulated by the Byzantine and Arab authorities, is amply attested in our sources.

Until Justinian II's minting of the imperial gold coinage with the image of Christ on it at the end of the 7th century, the Byzantine authorities appear to have supplied the Arab frontier zones with gold coinage and bronze for the minting of low-denomination issues. In return for this, according to our Islamic sources, the Muslims supplied the Byzantines with papyrus from Egypt. In the 10th century, as we have seen, Arab traders (especially in textiles) are recorded to have been resident in Constantinople, and a great deal of Byzantine–Arab trade was also conducted (albeit largely by Armenian middlemen) at the Black Sea trading post of Trebizond.

Beyond such 'high-level' and regulated transactions, there are also likely to have been autonomous patterns of exchange that developed at the grass roots of frontier society. As already indicated, the frontier was not an impermeable one, and consisted more of shaded areas of control rather than discrete territorial blocs. Given the nature of the frontier, in spite of differences of religion and the experience of warfare, it would only have been natural for the inhabitants of the Byzantine zones of control and those of the Muslim ones (many of whom remained Christian) to form reciprocal relations.

In particular, the great economic prosperity of the cities under Arab control would have acted as a magnet to those wishing to sell goods or seeking employment. The Arab historian Ibn al-Atir, for example, recorded that in the year 928 around 700 Byzantines and Armenians arrived in the Arab-held city of Melitene with pickaxes, seeking employment as labourers. It is, perhaps, less significant that these 'workmen' transpired to be Byzantine soldiers in disguise, than it is that this was regarded as convincing cover.

Moreover, by the 10th century society in Byzantium's eastern marchlands had come to be dominated by families of magnate warlords often of Armenian, Caucasian, or even Christian Arab descent, who had led local resistance to the invaders. In terms of culture and *mores*, such families had much in common with their Armenian, Kurdish, and Muslim Arab counterparts in enemy-held territory. There were close similarities, for example, in architectural style between elite residences in Byzantine Cappadocia and those in Arab-ruled northern Syria. Such marcher families were capable of forging cross-border alliances: a number of Arab warlords, for example, are recorded to have defected to Byzantium, while in 979 the eastern magnate Bardas Skleros fled to the caliphate when he failed to depose the Emperor Basil II.

There was also a market in brides that spanned the frontier zone. Thus the mythical hero of a tradition of Byzantine heroic poetry set in the world of the eastern marchlands, Digenis Akrites, is attested to have been of mixed parentage, half-Roman and half-Arab (his name literally meaning 'half-caste' or 'of double ancestry'). The literary and archaeological evidence combined, therefore, would suggest the gradual emergence of a relatively fluid frontier society, characterized by strong economic and personal ties that transcended the political and religious divide.

The vicissitudes of war

From their capital at Damascus, the caliphs of the Umayyad dynasty such as Abd al-Malik had effectively run what could be termed a '*jihad* state', the primary focus of which was the active pursuit of warfare against Byzantium. In the middle of the 8th century, however, the caliphate was torn apart by a civil war which witnessed the downfall of the Umayyads and their replacement by a new dynasty known as the Abbasids, who primarily drew their support from the formerly Persian territories to the east, where conversion to Islam had been at its most rapid, and where the decision of the Umayyads to levy taxes on Muslim converts which were only meant to be paid by Christians, Jews, and Zoroastrians had led to rising tensions.

As a result, the Abbasids chose to rule not from Syria, but rather from Iraq, in much greater geographical proximity to their natural centres of support. From their new capital at Baghdad, the Abbasid caliphs would survey a political horizon that looked east to Afghanistan and India, and north to the Caucasus, the Caspian, and the Steppe, as much as it did west to Byzantium. Consequently, the *jihad* against Constantinople ceased to be of the same order of priority to the caliphal authorities, and pressure on Byzantium's eastern frontier gradually began to ease.

Moreover, the Abbasid revolution of the mid-8th century also set in motion a more general process of fragmentation within the Islamic world. While North Africa and Spain (which had been conquered in the late 7th and early 8th centuries) remained loyal to members of the Umayyad clan, separate, free-standing regimes emerged in Egypt and elsewhere, where ongoing conversion to Islam among the subject populations allowed rulers and ruled to increasingly identify with one another, facilitating the emergence of more regionally focused power blocs, which continued to pay lip service to caliphal authority while operating with a growing degree of independence.

A further vicious struggle for power within the Abbasid heartland of Iraq at the end of the 9th century would leave the regime effectively hollowed out from within, meaning that, from then on, Byzantium no longer had to contend with a united Islamic foe on its eastern frontier. Rather, the leadership of the *jihad* against Constantinople increasingly passed to frontier commanders such as the *emirs* of Aleppo. Although volunteers from throughout the Muslim world continued to flock to northern Syria to participate in warfare against the infidel, such commanders were typically reliant on much smaller armies than the massed caliphal ranks of old. By virtue of this ongoing fragmentation of the Islamic world, therefore, the balance of power on the ground began to shift in favour of Byzantium.

A relative stabilization of military conditions on Byzantium's eastern frontier first becomes apparent in the reign of the iconoclast emperor Constantine V (and helps to explain in part his reputation for military success). The East Roman authorities initially took advantage of the easing of pressure to the east to engage in further internal reform, and to begin to reassert imperial control over mainland Greece and the southern Balkans (on which see Chapter 5).

At the same time, the new military circumstances permitted Byzantium the opportunity not only to contain but increasingly to surmount its 7th-century crisis. No longer disturbed by almost annual raids, the empire's urban and agrarian economy began to show signs of renewed vigour, while the final fading away of the bubonic plague from the reign of Constantine V onwards allowed population levels once more to begin to rise.

The *kastra*—the fortified military redoubts from which the *strategoi* or generals of the themes had exercised their authority— increasingly became the locus for bustling market fairs (*panegyreis*) which helped to stimulate agricultural and artisanal activity in the surrounding countryside. This facilitated a return to a higher level of monetization within the economy more generally. Soldiers who hitherto had received a cash bonus from the emperor only once every three or four years now received a yearly cash wage, further catalysing economic growth and the beginning of a return to late antique levels of sophistication in the more war-torn parts of the empire where it had been lost.

The increased sophistication of the Byzantine economy evident from the late 9th century was mirrored in the administrative and military spheres. The number of provincial themes was increased, allowing for still tighter administration, and within the themes there is evidence for the reassertion of the authority of civil magistrates. An administrative system that had initially been forged in the blistering heat of the struggle for military survival was now increasingly settling down into more regular, less crisis-driven ways. The less the military situation came to be predicated on the needs of defensive guerrilla warfare across much of western Anatolia and Asia Minor, the more the thematic infantry armies of these regions seem to have taken on an increasingly 'home guard' quality, morphing into local militias, perhaps mobilized periodically for occasional exercises, but less and less experienced in active warfare.

By the late 9th century the military and political fragmentation of the Islamic world was such that Byzantine emperors could seriously consider going on the offensive, and beginning to claw back territory that had last seen Roman banners under Heraclius and his dynasty. Such campaigns of territorial aggrandizement were best served primarily by cavalry rather than infantry forces.

The origins of this expansionist phase in Byzantine–Arab warfare can be traced back to the year 863, when a formidable Arab force was routed at Poson on the Halys river in Anatolia. From that moment on, Byzantine military endeavours appear to have taken on an ever-more aggressive aspect. By the early 10th century, Byzantine armies led by members of the eastern magnate families, characterized by their knowledge of the local terrain and with generations of accumulated experience of Byzantine–Arab warfare behind them, were ready to begin to advance into Armenia and Arab-held territory in Cilicia and northern Syria. Thus in the 930s the Byzantine general John Curcuas led victorious Byzantine forces into the cities of Melitene and Samosata, and began to strike beyond the Euphrates.

In 961 the Emperor Nicephorus Phocas (who himself belonged to an eastern marcher family) conquered the strategically vital island of Crete. By 965 Tarsus had fallen to the Romans and Cyprus had been annexed, while in 969 Antioch and Aleppo were conquered. By the time of the accession of Basil II in 976, Byzantine control extended into Syria, where the Emperor John Tzimisces (969–76) had led imperial forces in 975.

Soon Byzantine power would be projected northwards to the Caucasus with the annexation of Georgia (1000) and Armenia (1022), while to the west the empire would eventually eradicate the Bulgar state (1001–18), which had emerged in the northern Balkans in the aftermath of the collapse of Avar power in the 7th century, and which had seriously contested Byzantine control even over the immediate Thracian hinterland of Constantinople. In 1038 the Byzantines were able to prise Messina in Sicily from the Arabs, signalling a strengthening of the remaining imperial position in southern Italy.

By the early 11th century, therefore, Byzantium had staged an impressive comeback and was once more what it had last been at the end of the 6th century: the greatest power in Christendom. This had been achieved by ensuring that territory was clawed back from the Arabs in a gradual and piecemeal fashion, one city and its hinterland at a time.

Emperors appear to have been alert to the fact that it was primarily the disunity of their opponents that had presented them with the opportunity to expand once more and regain rightfully Roman territory. In particular, they avoided striking at prestige targets such as Baghdad or Jerusalem even when these prizes were potentially within reach, perhaps for fear that in doing so they would unite the Islamic world in a concerted *jihad* for which the Byzantines knew they would be no match. After four centuries of near constant warfare with the forces of Islam, the empire knew its foe too well to make that sort of error. Like all pugilists punching above their weight, emperors had to ensure that their blows were carefully targeted.

Chapter 5
Strategies for survival

History and diplomacy

Given the depth of the crisis into which Byzantium had been plunged by first the Persian and then the Arab conquests of the 7th century, the empire's ability to surmount its early medieval crisis, and to begin to reassert imperial power to both east and west by the early 10th century, is striking testimony to the effectiveness, pragmatism, and creativity of Byzantine statecraft at this time. In particular, the imperial authorities had managed to rapidly reorientate themselves in a fast-changing strategic landscape, and alter diplomatic and military priorities accordingly.

This ability had first been demonstrated at the end of the 4th century, when the authorities in Constantinople had found themselves faced with the threat posed by the Huns. The Huns appear to have originated in China, and from the mid-4th century had migrated westwards across the West Eurasian Steppe (the plains and grassland stretching from Manchuria to western Ukraine). They were remarkable horsemen and specialized in the use of a light composite bow which they deployed to deadly effect.

Although such steppe nomads were familiar to the Chinese, who had long ago learned to fear them, the late 4th century was the first time the Romans had ever encountered such a foe. They responded, as we have seen, by rapidly negotiating a peace with Persia, and by investing on a massive scale in the defences of Constantinople. But they also responded by analysing the Huns and attempting to learn from them by, for example, acquiring mercenaries with similar cavalry skills and emulating Hunnic forms of archery.

The Romans rapidly worked out that nomadic empires such as those of the Huns and the other steppe people who came in their wake in the 6th and 7th centuries (such as the Avars and Turks) were primarily held together by the prestige of the ruling *khagan* and the fear with which he was regarded by his subjects. All one had to do, Byzantine military handbooks of the 6th century had advised, was fight such foes to a standstill, and their power would rapidly collapse. This maxim had been vividly demonstrated before the walls of Constantinople in 626, when the failure of the Avar siege had led the *khagan*'s Slav conscripts to desert.

The Byzantines had emerged from the 5th and 6th centuries, therefore, with a keen appreciation of the empire's strategic sensitivity to developments on the West Eurasian Steppe, and the need to have allies in place to contain or contest the military pretensions of any new steppe power that emerged. Thus the imperial authorities were careful to maintain garrisons to act as 'listening-posts' on the Steppe in the northern Caucasus, and in Cherson and Crimea on the Black Sea.

Heraclius, as we have seen, had also identified in the dominant power on the West Eurasian Steppe a solution to his Persian crisis. It was a critical misfortune for the empire that the power of Heraclius' Turkic allies had waned at just the moment when they were needed against the Arabs. Nevertheless, emperors from the late 7th century were careful to ally themselves with the Khazars, whose empire replaced that of the late antique Turks to the north of the Caucasus and eastern Ukraine, thereby preventing the

Arabs from being able to advance across the region and strike at Byzantium from the Western Steppe and northern Balkans. Only the destruction of the Khazars by the descendants of Viking settlers known as the Rus' in the late 10th century would bring that alliance to an end, thereby unwittingly opening the way to the Islamicization of the northern Caucasus.

Likewise, the Byzantine authorities had analysed the power of the new barbarian kingdoms of the west, and correctly diagnosed the dynastic nature of power within them. Thus Justinian had struck at Vandal Africa, Ostrogothic Italy, and Visigothic Spain at moments of disputed succession to the throne, when such king-focused societies were at their weakest, and Byzantine rulers of the 8th, 9th, and 10th centuries would be keen to elicit diplomatic and military support by negotiating royal marriages for themselves and their kin.

When Byzantium's great western rivals of the era, the Carolingians and Ottonians, who had contested Byzantine authority in Italy and the Adriatic, themselves fragmented along dynastic lines, the imperial authorities were again primed to take advantage of the situation. What this shows is that, even though many of the offices of the Byzantine state had changed dramatically between the 6th century and the 10th, a tradition of analysis had been maintained, and was consistently deployed to the empire's military and political benefit.

This tradition was most clearly expressed in a fascinating work originating from the court of the Emperor Constantine VII (913–59) known as the *De Administrando Imperio* (or [Treatise] 'On How to Run the Empire'). The preface to the work is composed in the emperor's voice and it is dedicated to his son, the future Emperor Romanus II (959–63). Its purpose, Constantine declared, was to explain to the prince 'in what ways each foreign nation has power to benefit the Romans, and in what ways to harm them, and how and by what other nation each in turn may be encountered in arms and subdued'. The text itself is a compilation of extracts from historians and imperial biography, intelligence reports concerning foreign powers related back to the imperial authorities by eyewitnesses and merchants, and largely legendary accounts of migrations and former dealings between Byzantium and its neighbours aimed at emphasizing imperial claims to authority, alongside antiquarian details concerning Roman monuments meant to back these up.

At the same time, the treatise provides a relatively up-to-date account of imperial policy with respect to the Christian princes of the strategically crucial region of the Caucasus (i.e. Armenia and Georgia) and an analysis of how the major contemporary powers on the West Eurasian Steppe, the Danubian basin, and in the northern Balkans (Khazars, Rus', Pechenegs, Magyars, and Bulgars) related to and, crucially, could be turned against one another.

Thus, the work advises,

> to the Bulgarians, the emperor of the Romans will appear more formidable, and can impose on them the need for tranquility, if he is at peace with the Pechenegs, because the said Pechenegs are neighbours to those Bulgarians also, and, when they wish, either for private gain or to do a favour to the emperor of the Romans, they can easily march against Bulgaria...and overwhelm and defeat them.

Should they be unreliable, however, we are told, 'the Uzes can attack the Pechenegs'. As ever, 'divide and rule' was perceived to be the key to imperial survival.

The legacy of antiquity

Byzantium's ability to punch above its weight diplomatically was also enhanced by certain of its other inheritances from late antiquity. First, in the 6th century the empire had learned (above all with respect to the Caucasus) how conversion to imperial Christianity could be used to draw neighbouring peoples into an increasingly Constantinopolitan orbit. This lesson was not lost on emperors of the medieval period, who made concerted efforts to ensure that first the Serbs and Slavs settled in and around Greece, and then the Bulgars and Rus' (the latter with their capital at Kiev) adopted Christianity in its Byzantine form.

Those Slavs resident in Greece appear to have been evangelized in Greek, and thus became Hellenized in the course of their conversion (which proceeded alongside the restoration of direct imperial control). The adoption of imperial Christianity by the Bulgar *khagan* Boris (who took the baptismal name of Michael) in 864 had to be more carefully handled, as the Franks were also attempting to persuade him to embrace Christianity in its Latin form, and thereby to draw him into an anti-Byzantine Frankish axis. The imperial authorities responded by allowing Boris to establish an autonomous Bulgarian Church, with its own patriarch, and to receive a liturgy and Bible in the predominant language of his subjects (Old Church Slavonic). These texts originated in the work of two missionary brothers from Thessalonica, SS Cyril and Methodius, who were the favoured agents of imperial religious policy in eastern central Europe.

The Rus', whose Tsar Vladimir converted in 989, were, as we saw in Chapter 2, overwhelmed by the ritual, ceremonial, and architectural splendour of Hagia Sophia, such that they believed they had experienced the presence of God. The Rus' leader is reported to have previously considered converting not only to Latin Christianity, but also to Judaism and Islam. The latter, it is claimed, he had rejected on the grounds that 'drinking [alcohol] is the joy of the Rus". His conversion to Christianity in its Byzantine form served to lock the world of medieval Russia (like that of medieval Bulgaria) into what has been termed a 'Byzantine commonwealth', which allowed for the projection of 'soft power' and cultural influence at times when more direct inducements to cooperation with Constantinople were lacking.

As the conversion of the Rus' reminds us, imperial and religious ceremonial derived from late antiquity could also be deployed to secure tangible political gains. Sources such as the *Book of Ceremonies* and accounts written by foreign envoys record how the imperial authorities sought to manipulate and ritually choreograph diplomatic encounters to convey the full majesty of the emperor and Byzantium's cultural and technological superiority over its neighbours and rivals.

Particular emphasis appears to have been placed in such encounters on the role of the mechanical devices in which the Byzantines excelled. So, for example, in the 10th century the Italian diplomat Liudprand of Cremona records how, when he was presented to Constantine VII, on either side of the imperial throne mechanical lions had roared, synthetic birds chirped, and while he was made to prostrate himself before the dais, the imperial seat was raised on high as if by magic. 'How this was achieved,' he declares, 'I could not imagine'.

Such ceremonial could evidently be highly time-consuming. On a subsequent visit to Constantinople, Liudprand's conversation with the Emperor Nicephorus Phocas had to be cut short. As Liudprand writes 'At that moment a bell sounded. "It is past seven o'clock", said Nicephorus, "and there is a church procession which I must attend."'

Whatever the burden it imposed, however, such ceremonial formed an essential component of the Byzantine ideological arsenal. It was an important element of the accumulated resources of prestige and *savoir faire* that distinguished it from all other contemporary powers with which it found itself in direct conflict (with the possible exception of the Abbasids in Baghdad, who revived Sasanian forms of court ceremonial for similar purposes).

At the same time, despite the struggle over icons, the medieval Empire of Byzantium inherited from late antiquity a striking degree of ideological unity, focused not on any one imperial dynasty, but rather on the office of emperor and the concept of empire. As a result, the ideology of empire framed and determined the ambitions even of the most self-seeking aristocrats and generals, who typically aspired to obtain imperial power rather than to escape from it by carving out their own autonomous fiefdoms.

Again, this focus was culturally cemented through elaborate rituals at court whereby the emperor personally issued donatives and gifts to provincial potentates and *strategoi*, who were summoned to the capital, and with whom he dined at sumptuous feasts. Byzantine culture was also highly integrative politically. Through adoption of imperial Christianity and the acquisition of the Greek language, in particular, Roman identity could be relatively rapidly acquired. The 11th-century Byzantine general and man of letters Cecaumenos, for example, was a proud and patriotic Roman who bore an impeccably Greek name ('the burnt one') despite the fact that he was probably of Armeno-Georgian descent.

New crises and new solutions

Relations between the imperial government and the aristocracy were not, however, entirely straightforward. Rather as in late antiquity, the economic expansion of the 10th century fuelled the expansion of large estates. By virtue of this, members of the palatine aristocracy and the eastern magnate families increasingly acquired lands on which military service was owed, thereby threatening to undermine the thematic armies. This elicited a rash of legislation under emperors from Romanus Lecapenus (who ruled jointly with the young Constantine VII Porphyrogenitus from 920–44) to Basil II, who crushed a revolt by members of the eastern aristocracy, as a result of which, as we have seen, the leader of the attempted coup Bardas Skleros fled to Baghdad. Basil only achieved his victory, however, with outside help, his army bolstered by members of the 'Varangian guard' recruited from the Scandinavian Rus' of Kiev.

Although, as noted earlier, the Byzantine Empire was not a dynastic empire, for much of the period from the late 9th century through to the mid-11th the imperial title was held by members of the same bloodline, the so-called 'Macedonian' dynasty, so-named after Basil I 'The Macedonian' (867–86). In the 11th century, the courtier and scholar Michael Psellus wrote of it 'I believe no family has been favoured by God as theirs has been'.

Basil I himself was a pretty rum character, whose early career can perhaps best be characterized as that of a bit of rough turned high-class gigolo. As a young man of lowly background, he had attracted the patronage of a fantastically wealthy widow by the name of Danielis, whose favourite he became. Through Danielis, he was introduced to circles at court, and soon became close intimates with the dissolute young Emperor Michael III ('the Drunkard') who was, if anything, even more devoted to Basil than Danielis had been, and whom he appointed co-emperor. Basil repaid Michael for his kindness by having him assassinated and usurping his throne. It was a meteoric and eye-opening ascendancy that serves to remind one of the court-centred nature of the Byzantine polity.

Not all of Basil I's heirs took after the founder of their dynasty, and, for the early and mid-10th century, we should note in particular the reign of Constantine VII Porphyrogenitus, who followed in the footsteps of his father Leo VI (886–912) in encouraging a revival of learning and letters, sponsoring an encyclopaedic movement that aimed to codify and order human knowledge relating to fields ranging from foreign policy and court ceremonial to horse medicine, and engaging in the construction of prestigious architectural monuments.

This movement, once known to scholars as the 'Macedonian Renaissance', was clearly on some level a political statement: it was a response to and refutation of both the Carolingian Renaissance of the west of the 8th and 9th centuries, and the contemporaneous patronage of learning and the arts evident at the court of the Abbasid Caliphs of Baghdad. Just as the Byzantine emperor surpassed all other temporal rulers on earth in terms of authority, so too should his court excel theirs in terms of culture. The movement also attempted to reconnect culturally and ideologically with the age of Justinian, so as to extirpate the memory of the iconoclasts.

The last ruler of the Macedonian dynasty died in 1066, and there followed a period of political uncertainty which witnessed a marked reversal in Byzantine fortunes. It was to be another twenty-five years or so before Byzantium regained something approximating to the relative dynastic stability it had enjoyed under the Macedonians. In 1081 the imperial title was usurped by Alexius I Comnenus, members of whose kin were to hold the imperial office until 1185, when the throne was in turn seized by Isaac II Angelos (1185–95), his brother Alexius III (1195–1203), and his son Alexius IV, who was murdered by Alexius V who was in turn deposed by the Fourth Crusade in 1204.

These rulers—the Comnenoi and Angeloi—ruled over an empire living in much more straitened circumstances than had prevailed at the death of Basil II in 1025, when Byzantium had reached its medieval apogee in terms of territory and political clout (see Map 5). The reasons for this lay primarily in events beyond the empire's control. If external developments had facilitated the expansion of the empire in the 9th and 10th centuries, a further reconfiguration of the world beyond Byzantium ultimately did much to undo those gains.

The most immediate threat faced by the empire in the 11th century was that posed by the Pechenegs, a highly rapacious and

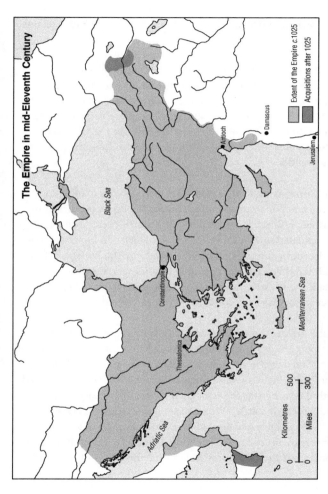

Map 5. The empire in the mid-11th century.

militarized nomadic tribal confederation cut from the same cloth as the Huns and Avars, who had come to dominate the Western Steppe in the late 9th century, and with whom, as we have seen, the *De Administrando Imperio* of Constantine VII had been much concerned.

Basil II's subjugation of Bulgaria had brought the empire into direct contact with these people. As a result, the Pechenegs emerged as the chief rival to Byzantium along the lower Danube. In 1033–6 the Pechenegs launched a series of devastating raids deep into imperial possessions in the Balkans, reaching as far as Thessalonica—the second city of the empire—in search of booty and plunder.

The imperial authorities responded with a series of measures that, in the medium term, served to contain the Pecheneg threat. In particular, through a drastic 'scorched earth' policy a deliberately depopulated *cordon sanitaire* was established in imperial territory to the south of the Danube to disincentivize the Pechenegs from raiding, while carefully regulated frontier markets were established at specific border garrison posts to provide the Pechenegs with such goods as they most desired.

A still greater threat to the integrity of Byzantium, however, was to emerge along its eastern frontier, where the empire found itself confronted by the new and formidable power of the Seljuk Turks. The Turks, likewise, were essentially steppe nomads, and shared with the Pechenegs the same high degree of mobility on horseback and ferocity in battle. With respect to the Seljuks, however, such warlike instincts had been given greater focus by their recent conversion to Islam. The traditional martial ethos of the steppe nomad was thus harnessed to the greater purpose of the *jihad*.

Under their leader Togrul and his successors Alp Arslan and Malik Shah, the Seljuks had come to dominate the Abbasid court, acting as the power behind the caliphal throne, and directing their nomadic Turkmen kin against the Christian populations of Georgia, Armenia, and Byzantium. Byzantine–Arab warfare, as we have seen, had hitherto operated on the basis of organized campaigns fought by similarly structured armies during a clearly identifiable campaigning season. The Seljuk-directed Turkmen, however, operated in smaller, highly mobile groups capable of circumventing imperial defences and outmanoeuvring Byzantine troops units. Lacking a central base or a clearly articulated command structure for the Byzantines to attack, containing the Turkmen threat on the eastern frontier was rather like attempting to hold liquid mercury: it was as futile an exercise as it was a dangerous one.

In 1071 the Emperor Romanus IV Diogenes launched an eastern offensive that brought him into direct conflict with the Seljuk Sultan Alp Arslan. At the Battle of Manzikert, the emperor was defeated and captured, leading to a civil war in Byzantium that permitted the Turks and Turkmen to advance deep into Anatolia and Asia Minor, where the now largely vestigial thematic armies were no longer fit for purpose. Within just twenty years, the Turks had established themselves on the western coast of Asia Minor and were beginning to settle. The most economically developed region of the empire, where the sophisticated infrastructure of antiquity had been most fully preserved, was now rendered a warzone.

The more the Turks settled, however, the more feasible it became for the empire to strike back against them, and as early as the 1080s the Byzantine army began to inflict localized defeats on the Turks. A major problem faced by the Byzantine authorities, however, was that the imperial army appeared to lack the expertise in siege technology required to liquidate enemy strongholds such as Nicaea in the west or Antioch in the east. Without control of such cities, it would be impossible for the Byzantines to turn such victories into wars of territorial reconquest.

Some sort of solution to this situation emerged in the reign of Alexius I Comnenus, who, as noted earlier, seized the throne in 1081. The Seljuk and Turkmen advances into Anatolia and Asia Minor had led to an influx into the imperial capital of members of the Byzantine military aristocracy who had lost their estates to the enemy and were thus embittered against the imperial authorities. The emperor attempted to elicit their support by according members of the aristocracy extensive rights over communities of hitherto free taxpayers, from whom they were allowed to demand tribute and labour services in what effectively amounted to a 'feudal revolution' within Byzantium, completing the process of intensification of aristocratic control that had elicited such imperial concern in its earlier phases in the 10th century.

Alexius, however, was eager to his limit his political and military dependence on the aristocracy. As a result we see him increasingly turning to members of his own family to fill governmental posts, and, crucially, coming to rely on foreign, largely western mercenaries and knights to supplement the imperial guard.

By the early 11th century, as we have seen, Byzantium had re-established its position as the dominant power in Christendom. The consequent prestige and wealth of the Byzantine emperor had led many members of western, and especially French knightly families eager for adventure, to enter into imperial service through joining the imperial guard. Alexius was keen to foster this development, even engaging Norman knights in his service in spite of the role played by the Normans in the mid-11th century in undermining the Byzantine position in Sicily, Southern Italy, and the Adriatic. For, importantly, such knights possessed precisely the expertise in siege warfare that the empire most needed.

Accordingly, in 1095, Alexius approached Pope Urban II to issue an appeal to the Latin West for military aid, as a result of which the Pope issued a call to arms, declaring a Crusade against the

Muslim infidels to liberate the Christians of the East and restore Christian control over the Holy Land. In the following two years around 60,000 westerners would make their way to Constantinople to bolster the empire's cause.

The first bands of crusaders to arrive appear to have been made up primarily of peasants and other relatively poorly equipped troops whom the emperor quickly shipped over to Asia Minor, where they soon met a grisly end. As the more disciplined and experienced contingents of knightly crusaders arrived, however, the imperial authorities were careful to direct them to the cities in Asia Minor and Syria that they most needed to prise from enemy hands.

In 1097 the Seljuk base of Nicaea fell, and the crusading army proceeded to march on to Antioch. The initial attempt on this city, however, faltered. As a result, on the advice of the Crusade's own leaders, Alexius ordered the imperial army to withdraw. The subsequent fall of the city to the Norman adventurer Bohemond served to sour relations between the crusaders and the imperial government when Bohemond refused to cede the territory.

The breaking point in relations between Alexius and the crusading leadership, however, came when the latter determined to press onwards to Jerusalem, and expected Alexius to march with them. This the emperor was never going to do. Whereas Jerusalem had emerged as a major focus of devotion and pilgrimage in the western Church, in Byzantium, as we have seen, the city of Constantinople had come to be reimagined as a sort of New Jerusalem, thereby decentring the prototype.

Consequently, the imperial authorities were unable to share the westerners' enthusiasm to march on the holy city. Moreover, as noted earlier, even at the height of imperial expansion in the early 11th century the imperial government had been careful not to strike at Jerusalem (which was also holy to Muslims) or Baghdad, for fear of sparking off a concerted *jihad*. The crusading leadership, by contrast, were oblivious to this danger and interpreted Alexius' reticence as betrayal. When, therefore, in 1098 Jerusalem fell, it (like Antioch) became the seat of an independent Latin kingdom under crusader control.

The differing character of eastern and western Christian piety as it had emerged over the course of the early Middle Ages thus led to misunderstanding and recrimination. To a certain degree, Alexius' solution to the Seljuk threat had backfired (although it was still better from an imperial perspective to have the crusaders in control of Antioch than the Muslims).

It is important to appreciate, however, that Alexius and his successors never entirely gave up on the idea that the piety, ambition, and martial spirit of the Latin West could be harnessed to serve the empire's purposes. Thus repeated efforts were made to manipulate the territorial ambitions of the German emperors to contain the Norman presence in Italy, while Byzantium increasingly drew upon the mercantile Italian city states such as Venice or Amalfi (nominally vassals and subjects of the emperor) to bolster its navy.

It was this that led Alexius and his Comnenian successors to concede to the Italians significant trading rights in the imperial capital, including tax-exemption and the establishment of colonies of merchants on the Golden Horn. This would lead to a dramatic increase in the number of westerners resident in the imperial capital, as well as growing Italian dominance of the mercantile and commercial sectors of the empire's economy.

The continuing, active involvement of Latin traders, knights, and adventurers in imperial affairs was to be of lasting significance. For it meant that, as a result, the German emperors, the crusaders, and the Italian merchants became drawn into the internal politics of the empire, leading to growing resentment against them on the part of elements within the Byzantine governing classes and the inhabitants of the imperial capital.

In particular, the crusaders and representatives of the Italian city states were increasingly caught up in the factional disputes that beset the Comnenian family at the end of the 12th century, and the usurpation and subsequent series of struggles for the throne resulting from the deposition of the Comnenoi by the Angeloi in 1185.

This drawing of the west into the factional politics of the Byzantine court was to culminate in 1204, when the Fourth Crusade (initially directed at Egypt) was rerouted to Constantinople, where the son of the deposed emperor Isaac II Angelos promised its leaders huge sums of money in return for helping him to gain the throne. When the duly elevated Emperor Alexius V was unable to pay them, however, the crusaders sacked the city amid an orgy of violence, and established their own regime under the leadership of Count Baldwin of Flanders. It would prove to be a devastating blow.

Chapter 6
Text, image, space, and spirit

Culture and conservatism

Byzantine imperial ideology, as we have seen, was predicated upon the concept of the absolute historical continuity of the Roman state and the rigid immutability of the emperor's claim to authority over all rightly Roman territory. The disparity between the fraught military fortunes of the empire across much of its medieval history, as compared to its late antique past, often lent imperially sponsored works of art and acts of cultural patronage a strongly conservative and atavistic quality.

The emperors of the iconoclast period (especially Constantine V), for example, sought to reconnect to the age of Constantine the Great, replacing religious images in churches with the symbol of the Cross which had appeared to Constantine prior to his victory at the Battle of the Milvian Bridge in 312. Likewise, as we have seen, the emperors of the Macedonian dynasty had attempted to reconnect with the era of Justinian in an effort to obliterate the memory of the recent iconoclast past. As a result, 'renewal' (*kainourgia*) and 'cleansing' (*anakatharsis*) were imperial bywords: 'innovation' was not.

This profoundly conservative ideological impulse informed a broader tendency towards conservatism in Byzantine literary culture, which was a legacy from antiquity. Educated Byzantines inherited from the Roman Empire of the era of the 'Second Sophistic' (a movement of literary efflorescence that took place in the Greek-speaking east when it was initially subjected to Roman rule) the belief that all high literature of a non-instructional and non-devotional sort should be written in Attic (i.e. the Greek of Classical Athens, as preserved and studied by the Second Sophistic scholars).

Thus, in the 6th century the contemporary historian Procopius had largely modelled his prose style and vocabulary on that of the Athenian historian Thucydides, whose *History of the Peloponnesian War* had been penned over a thousand years earlier. This adoption of the 'high style' not only obliged Procopius to handle grammatical forms that were no longer current in spoken Greek, but also to try to avoid neologisms. Words that did not form part of the inherited classical vocabulary could not be used in polite literature. Instead, the ancient terminology had to be stretched to embrace contemporary developments.

So, for example, when describing Hagia Sophia Procopius could not describe it as an *ekklesia* ('church'), as in Attic that term had signified an assembly. Instead, he adopted the word *naos,* really meaning 'temple', but which the *diktats* of the 'high style' deemed more acceptable.

Down to the end of the Byzantine Empire, and long thereafter, therefore, Greek authors who aspired to write *belles-lettres* were obliged to do so in an ossified linguistic register and on the basis of largely static literary models ultimately derived from Athens *circa* the 5th century BC. This had the advantage that those ancient Greek authors whom Byzantine schoolmasters and copyists regarded as models of good Attic style, or whom the Athenians had come to hold in high regard, would be preserved for posterity. Such classroom texts of the Byzantine Empire literally became the Greek 'classics' as they would be transmitted to the Humanists of the Renaissance and Early Modern West. Without this backward-glancing dimension to Byzantine literary culture, the works of Aristotle, Plato, Herodotus, Thucydides, Aeschylus, and Sophocles would all have been lost (or, in the case of Aristotle, would only have partially survived in translation).

The cultural price of this for Byzantium itself was that Byzantine literary high culture effectively constituted what has been described as a 'literature of display', whereby authors typically sought to strip their compositions of anything that gave them local colour, personality, or novelty. An author's artistry was demonstrated above all by his conformity to a literary language and models that were almost completely irrelevant and incomprehensible to those outside of the *belle-lettriste* culture (thereby often rendering anonymous works almost impossible to date).

This necessarily meant that the readership for even the finest of such compositions could be extremely limited. In the age of Justinian, the education required to understand Attic was demanded for entry into the imperial government, and was aspired to by members of the local elite across the cities of the empire as a whole. Indeed, Procopius tells us that his *History of the Wars* was read in every corner of the Roman world.

It is striking, however, that almost every work of history written in Greek in the 'high style' in late antiquity appears to have been written in Constantinople, implying that it was in the imperial capital that the bulk of sufficiently educated readers (and audiences for the declamation of such texts) was really to be found. The urban destruction wrought by first Persian and then Arab warfare in the 7th and 8th centuries, however, led to massive cultural dislocation. With the destruction of many of the cities of the empire, and the dramatic shrivelling of those that survived, much of the old educational infrastructure was swept away. The provincial *locus* for the replication of traditional elite culture was no more. As a result much of the provincial readership for texts written in the 'high style' disappeared.

Only in Constantinople is a traditional literary education likely to have remained available across the vicissitudes of the period, but even there the educational infrastructure was highly limited and subject to the shifting priorities of different regimes, meaning that the number of readers capable of truly appreciating the Atticizing literature of the 10th and 11th centuries probably amounted to just a few hundred in any one generation.

The urban revival of the Comnenian period may have witnessed the growth of a larger, more bourgeois audience. Nevertheless, it has still been suggested that, in the 13th century, the historian Nicetas Choniates (who wrote a moving account of the fall of Constantinople to the Fourth Crusade) may have known all of his readers *by name*.

Byzantine literary culture also inherited from that of the Second Sophistic a strong interest in rhetorical texts, such as had formed the basis of the higher stages of secondary education in the Roman Empire. With their elaborate rules and fixed conventions as to how individuals were to be praised, buildings described, and cities lauded, the predilection for such works served to further distance classicizing texts from Byzantine realities.

Byzantine literature, it has been noted, thus had something of the character of a 'distorting mirror' about it, presenting an Atticized view of a profoundly unclassical world. Unlike the fairground attraction from which that simile is derived, however, the primary aim was to display intellectual refinement.

'Honey from a whore's lips'

The strongly conservative inflection to Byzantine culture was further intensified by the influence of the Church. As pagan critics of Christianity took great pleasure in noting, the core texts of the Christian New Testament had not been written in the 'high style' appropriate to noble and lofty thoughts. Rather, they had been written in the common Greek (*koine*) that had become the *lingua franca* of the Near East during the Hellenistic period. As a result, there would always be an element within the Church that regarded 'Greek learning' as irrelevant: all the pious Christian needed was his Bible.

Thus, for example, in the 6th century, an historian from Antioch known as John Malalas wrote a history covering the period from the Creation to the present day that displayed almost no interest in the history of Greece and Rome, save insofar as it coincided with Biblical history or revealed God's plan for mankind. It was, moreover, written in a plain style, much closer to the spoken Greek of the day, and was structured on the basis of literary allusions that were entirely Biblical in nature. Likewise, Malalas' close contemporary, the eccentric Alexandrian merchant Cosmas, penned a 'Christian Topography', full of garbled details of the flora and fauna of distant regions, which was intended to reveal that the structure of the physical world conformed to the design of the Biblical tabernacle.

The message from both authors was clear: only 'Bible learning' was true learning. Malalas and Cosmas had their pagan equivalent in the Emperor Julian (361–3) who had decided, during his literary studies, that intellectual Hellenism and Christianity were ultimately incompatible. Given the choice between 'the Nazarene' (as he termed Christ) and Homer, Julian had chosen Homer.

Political and cultural conditions, however, necessitated that the likes of Malalas and Cosmas were progressively sidelined. In late antiquity, the awareness of a common high culture rooted in the study of Homer, Thucydides, Herodotus, and the rest of the Greek canon, and the linguistic unity associated with the common aspiration to Attic style, had served to unite the Greek-speaking elite of members of Rome's eastern provinces and had become central to their self-identity. If the Constantinian and post-Constantinian Church were to be fully integrated and institutionalized (as many of its leaders desired), it would have to reconcile itself to Greek high culture in general, and Greek literature in particular.

Thus, in the 4th century, St Basil of Caesarea wrote a treatise justifying the pursuit by Christians of a traditional literary and rhetorical education, which provided the young mind with the preparation required to accept the higher truths. While some critics regarded Greek learning as the proverbial 'honey that runs from the lips of the whore', the emphasis on style and rhetorical structure allowed Christians to eviscerate classical literature of its pagan contents and themes (which, in any case, could be understood in a Christian sense allegorically, with Hercules, for example, representing the Biblical David).

Instead, the analytical structures of Greek speculative philosophy were deployed by those in attendance at the Church Councils attempting to thrash out Trinitarian and Christological theology, while the great churchmen of the 4th and 5th centuries, such as John Chrysostom, delivered sermons that were perfectly crafted examples of ancient rhetoric. The Fathers of the Church thus reinforced the authority of the 'high style', while establishing the *koine* of the Greek Bible as a separate linguistic register better suited to communication with the mass of the faithful.

Likewise, in secular literature of a more instructional sort, a more demotic register was deemed appropriate. Thus, in the 10th century, the Emperor Constantine VII declared in the preface to his treatise *De Administrando Imperio*: 'I have not been studious to make a display of fine writing or of an Atticizing style, swollen with the sublime and lofty, but have rather been eager by means of everyday and conversational narrative to teach you those things of which you should not be ignorant.' The appreciation of such multiple registers is the key to understanding medieval Greek literature.

The Byzantine Church thus ultimately served to buttress the empire's highly conservative literary high culture. At the same time, however, it refashioned it. The homilies and writings of the Church Fathers, such as Chrysostom or Gregory of Nazianzus, became an important addition to the literary canon. Moreover, the institutional survival of the Church across the period of Byzantium's 7th-century crisis meant that ecclesiastical (and specifically monastic) scriptoria played perhaps the single most important role in the transmission of literary texts from the late antique world of the 6th century to the medieval world of the 8th.

This process of transmission was greatly facilitated by the development at the time of a 'minuscule' script, which meant that texts could be copied from papyrus (the main medium for writing in antiquity) to parchment (on which the empire had to rely once the Arabs began to cut off the papyrus supply from Egypt) at greater speed. This smaller, cursive script also meant that scribes could pack in more words per page, thereby reducing the costs of copying.

The centrality of Church scriptoria to textual transmission would have major consequences for the future development of Byzantine intellectual culture, as it meant that a great deal of secular literature of which the ecclesiastical authorities disapproved could be carefully set aside. Likewise, the fact that we know almost nothing of what late antique 'heretics' such as Arius or Nestorius actually wrote or preached save for what their opponents claimed, is probably less indicative of the effectiveness of late Roman autocracy than it is of the theological self-censorship of Byzantine scriptoria.

With the destruction of much of the civic landscape of the old empire, and the near obliteration of pre-Christian traditions of secular education, the Church had emerged as the dominant force within Byzantine literary culture, and much of the readership and audience for literary texts of all sorts that had re-emerged by the end of the 8th century was primarily monastic in character, with tastes and interests that were bound to marginalize the secular or the unconventional.

There were, inevitably, exceptions: historians are fortunate, for example, that the pagan Emperor Julian was regarded a sufficiently fine Attic stylist for his virulently anti-Christian writings to be carefully preserved by generations of Byzantine scribes.

Even including classical survivals, however, as a result of ecclesiastical domination of modes of textual transmission, the medieval Byzantine library would be an overwhelmingly ecclesiastical and Christian affair. It is a striking fact that almost 90 per cent of all extant Byzantine manuscripts identified as having originated from the period between the 9th and 11th centuries are religious in character.

This even impacted on the private collections (and, presumably, mental horizons) of literate men of the world, such as the 11th-century general Cecaumenos. Analysis suggests that his private library (much of which he may have inherited) comprised ten Biblical texts, thirty-three liturgical works, twelve monastic ones, three works of monastic spirituality, one example of *apocrypha*, four accounts of the lives of saints, two Christian miscellanies, three works on Church law, and ten volumes of 'secular' literature, including a grammar, a legal work, a couple of chronicles, a guide to dreams, and five ancient or late antique literary compositions.

Byzantium, as we have seen, played a vital role in the transmission and survival of the core texts of the ancient Greek literary canon. As a result of changing religious sensibilities and the cultural dislocation and physical destruction caused by warfare and civic strife, however, a great deal of literary, philosophical, and scientific writing would also fail to be transmitted.

In 476, for example, the great public library of Constantinople, built by Constantius II to house secular texts, burnt down with the reported loss of 120,000 volumes (probably meaning papyrus rolls). In the 9th century, the Patriarch of Constantinople and humanist Photius wrote up a series of notes and comments detailing his reading. These notes (known as the *Bibliotheca*) comprise 280 volumes detailing 386 works read, of which 233 were Christian and 147 secular or pagan. Just over half of these are now either totally lost or survive only in fragmentary form. The damage wrought to Constantinople by the Fourth Crusade (as well as the final Ottoman conquest of the city) is also likely to have led to the loss of many texts.

Images and the imagination

The conservative cultural influence of the Church, moreover, was not limited to literary culture. The debate over icons in the 8th and 9th centuries had led certain proponents of the pro-icon (or iconodule) party to fall back on an argument that was ultimately rooted in Greek philosophy of a late Platonic variety, namely that the images depicted on icons were an accurate depiction of the prototype (Christ, Mary, or the saint himself), and therefore that reverence shown to the image was reverence of the prototype rather than veneration of the image (and thus was not idolatrous).

In late antiquity, images of individual saints had come to develop key identifiable features which, beyond the written ascription, allowed the worshipper to identify precisely which holy or saintly figure was depicted in the image concerned: hence the Virgin Mary's instantly recognizable mode of attire. Especially in the post-iconoclast era, this necessarily limited the artist or artisan's room for manoeuvre. While, on the one hand, the logic of the argument that the icon represented a true image should have constituted an inducement to greater naturalism in religious art, in practice the emphasis on standard recognizable features allowed for a high degree of visual 'shorthand', such that any image of an old man with curly white hair and a hooked nose could fairly confidently be assumed to be of St Peter.

Moreover, the emphasis on the relation between image and 'real' prototype meant that the Church developed a keen hostility to the visual depiction (or even literary description) of things or beings that were not 'real', such as mythological beasts either inherited from antiquity or dreamed up by the artist or author concerned. The realm of the imagination was not one with which the Church felt comfortable, and an openness to the fantastical was interpreted as an invitation to the demonic.

This in turn appears to have led to an interesting shift in lay attitudes towards images of sphinxes, gryphons, and other hybrid characters derived from the world of classical mythology: whereas the (educated) late antique viewer may have been in a position to understand their literary origins and allusive qualities, medieval Byzantine observers of the inherited visual repertoire, it has been suggested, increasingly regarded such images as possessing a magical or talismanic quality, as a result of which one finds them depicted on amulets or painted on bowls, no longer as a sign of antiquarian taste, but rather so as to harness their magical power.

Necessity and innovation

It is vital to appreciate, however, that irrespective of a façade of continuity, the objective cultural context in which Byzantium operated across the centuries inevitably generated new cultural forms and acted as a spur to much greater creativity than has often been supposed. In spite of the grip of the 'high style' on the world of *belles-lettres*, this was even true with respect to Byzantine literature.

In late antiquity, for example, the rise of the Church and the development of Christianity led to the emergence of new forms of literature which would come to play an important role in the literary canon, over and beyond the homilies already mentioned. Foremost among these was that of hagiography, or accounts of the lives of Christian saints, initially written in a plain style (although in the Macedonian era a concerted move was made to elevate the linguistic register of such texts).

The first saint's life was that of the 3rd-century Egyptian hermit and father of monasticism St Anthony, written in Greek *c*. 360 by Athanasius, Patriarch of Alexandria. While drawing on existing traditions of secular biography, this text, with its vivid accounts of Anthony's struggle with the devil, played well to a late antique fascination with demonology, and was soon translated and emulated by a range of authors, such as Mark the Deacon in the 5th century, who penned a detailed account of the life of the 4th-century St Porphyrius of Gaza, or the monk George who, in the 7th century, composed a life of his contemporary St Theodore of Sykeon, which contains vivid scenes derived from the world of rural social relations.

Likewise, the rise of the Church sponsored novel approaches to the writing of history, epitomized by the Christian 'world chronicle' written by John Malalas which, as noted earlier, sought to chart the history of mankind from Creation to the present day, in anticipation of Divine Judgement and the Last Days. With its teleological view of history, and its sidelining of the Graeco-Roman past, Malalas' approach stood in radical opposition to that of his contemporary Procopius, whose *History of the Wars* fails to take an expressly Christian line on anything, and whose vision of the past was predicated on the glories of Greece and Rome.

These two authors reveal the existence of an early Byzantine 'culture war', which would only begin to be resolved by the gradual emergence of more expressly Christian forms of classicizing history at the end of the 6th century (such as that written by Agathias, who continued Procopius' task in charting the history of Justinian's campaigns). The liturgical development of the Church also helped to generate new literary forms. Thus, in 6th-century Constantinople, the cantor of the Great Church Romanos ('the Melode') wrote hymns in Greek in forms of verse derived from the Christian Semitic language of Syriac. This was literary innovation born of specifically late antique cultural encounters.

The world of secular literature was also undergoing interesting processes of change at this time. While those writing history in the 'high style' across the 6th and 7th centuries continued to aspire to write in Attic (and in the case of Procopius did so with considerable genius), one witnesses an increasingly daring and creative blend of literary forms.

Thus, although in his *History of the Wars*, Procopius relied heavily on Thucydides for his vocabulary, he also borrowed narrative structures from Arrian's account of the campaigns of Alexander, and embedded his analysis of Justinian's regime in a complex web of literary allusions. In his scurrilous *Secret History*, moreover, Procopius drew on the narrative structures derived from the world of the Greek novel and the vocabulary of comedy, while also inverting the codified rhetorical form of the panegyric or encomium (a speech or composition lauding an individual) to compose a startlingly original assault on Justinian, Theodora, and their entourage.

A similar recombination of literary genres is evident in the 7th century in the *History* composed by Theophylact Simocatta. Although a prose history in the high style, the narrative structure of this work was derived from the world of Greek tragedy, with the murdered Emperor Maurice the tragic hero. The *History* opens with a dialogue between the Muses of History and Philosophy, which a purist would have found even more disorientating. Theophylact's contemporary, the court historian

George of Pisidia, composed a history of Heraclius' Persian wars (which only survives in a fragmentary form) in which a prose account of the emperor's campaigns is interspersed with speeches delivered in verse. There is every sign here of an era of great literary creativity that first ground to a halt and was then swept away by the urban destruction and cultural dislocation of the 7th century.

In places and at times when the dead hand of Atticizing *belles-lettrist* culture was at its weakest, medieval Byzantine literature was also capable of developing in novel directions. As we have already seen with respect to the tradition of the *Digenis* poem, the military and social conditions on Byzantium's eastern frontier around the 10th century led to the spontaneous emergence of a tradition of heroic poetry which would be gradually refined in the 11th and 12th centuries, while the cultural encounter between Greek and Latin elites in the aftermath of the Fourth Crusade would lead to the composition in Greek of tales based on western vernacular chivalric romances.

In those parts of the Byzantine world (such as the Morea in Greece or the island of Cyprus) that would remain under Latin rule, the writing of historical chronicles would also develop in a quite distinct manner. Changing social contexts necessarily led to the emergence of new literary forms.

The relationship between innovation and necessity, however, is at its clearest with respect to Byzantine architectural and artistic development. As seen in Chapter 2 with regard to Constantinople, emperors after Justinian did not really have the economic resources available to build on the same sort of scale as the emperors of late antiquity. Imperial and aristocratic architectural commissions of the 8th, 9th, and 10th centuries thus had to be on a smaller scale and, interestingly, with respect to ecclesiastical architecture were built according to different architectural principles.

Such newly commissioned churches typically took the form of the 'cross in square' (a dome placed above four barrel vaults forming a Greek cross, placed within a square supported internally either by four columns or four sets of piers). In larger examples of this type, additional, subsidiary domes could be placed on each of the four arms of the cross around the central dome.

This design, it has been suggested, probably originated to serve the needs of small monastic communities (perhaps in Bithynia, near Constantinople, where there was an expansion of monasticism in the 8th century), but was soon adopted more generally as it was better suited to the needs of the shrunken congregations of the early medieval period than the cross-domed basilica of the Justinianic era, which could accommodate larger crowds. It was a pragmatic piece of downsizing which would, however, have implications for the future development of Orthodox forms of devotion.

For it should be noted that the dissemination of the new form of Byzantine ecclesiastical architecture also coincided with the struggle over images within the Byzantine Church, and, as a result, architectural and artistic developments would soon acquire an important synergy. The emperors of the iconoclast era, as we have seen, tended to decorate churches with crosses, or with scenes and patterns of flora and fauna that were meant to evoke the stylized mosaics of the grand basilica churches of the Constantinian era. Such styles were copied by members of the provincial aristocracy and are attested, for example, in the churches built by members of the military magnate elite in Cappadocia. Images of Christ, Mary, and the saints were eschewed (although they would later be added).

But in the truly grand imperial foundations of late antiquity such images had never played a central role: the internal spaces of such places of worship were so vast that it was far easier, quicker, and cheaper for the imperial authorities simply to cover the walls of these foundations with patterned mosaics (this was especially true of Hagia Sophia, which, as we have seen, was built in haste).

The iconoclast dispute, however, had made a great issue of images. As a result, in the aftermath of the victory of the iconodule party in 843, images were reintroduced to Byzantine churches on a far greater scale than had been the case before. Once again, beneath a rhetoric of restoration, genuine innovation was taking place. In 867, for example, the Patriarch Photius revealed an enormous (and exquisite) mosaic of the Virgin and Child in the eastern apse of Hagia Sophia (see Figure 6). In his homily on the occasion of the unveiling, Photius described the event as an act of restoration. In fact, no such image had ever stood there before. The role, significance, and visibility of the holy image had thus been dramatically enhanced.

In Hagia Sophia, the introduction of the mosaic image of the Virgin had a startling effect. But it remained, to some extent, tucked away amid the overall structure. In the smaller Byzantine churches that were the product of the early medieval period, however, the adoption of increasingly rich iconic schemes of decoration served to transform the psychological and emotive basis of Orthodox worship, as the shrunken interior of the churches, and the greater proximity between viewer and viewed, meant that saint and worshipper could now enter into a much more personal and direct relationship. Crucially, decoration in the form of figurative mosaic also became much more financially feasible as less surface space had to be covered. Accordingly, such decoration became the great glory of the Byzantine Church.

At the same time, the scheme of images within such places of worship became increasingly standardized (although never uniform). For the most part, the central dome was reserved for the image of Christ 'Pantokrator' ('the Ruler of All'), sometimes accompanied by saints and cherubim. In hierarchical descent, the semi-dome of the apse would tend to be accorded to the Virgin

6. Mosaic depiction of Virgin and Child from the apse of Hagia Sophia, unveiled by the Patriarch Photius in 867.

Mary, often in the company of the archangels Michael and Gabriel. Below Christ could be seen the Apostles and Prophets of the Old Testament; beneath Mary, the Communion of the Apostles and 'clerical' saints (such as John Chrysostom). The pendentives supporting the central dome were accorded to the four Evangelists, while the barrel vaults were given over to New Testament scenes. Finally, remaining wall surfaces in the nave were typically the preserve of groups of 'secular' saints such as the soldier saints George, Demetrius, and their fellows. This scheme can still essentially be used to read most Byzantine and Orthodox churches to this day.

The visual arts had never been abandoned as such in the iconoclast era. However, the growing emphasis on images and the arts more generally in the wake of iconoclasm posed certain problems. For the post-iconoclast emperors of the Macedonian dynasty attempted to reach back to the highly naturalist and expressive artistic traditions of the Justinianic period. Many of the skills needed to replicate and emulate that art, however, had been lost amid the warfare and urban dislocation of the 6th and 7th centuries. Accordingly, such skills had to be gradually relearned through the careful copying of late antique survivals.

This was a slow and painstaking process, and it was arguably only in the 11th and 12th centuries that the desired result was finally achieved, before developing in new directions in the 13th and 14th centuries (see Figure 7). Moreover, the great public context in which late antique art had existed had likewise largely disappeared with the destruction of the city in its ancient guise. As a result, images, and forms that had originated in the realm of late antique public art (such as scenes depicted on monumental friezes and columns) were transposed to more domestic and private contexts: above all manuscript illuminations, ivories, and enamels.

It is a striking fact, for example, that while the cities of late antiquity had been jam-packed with life-like and larger statues of

7. Mosaic depiction of Christ from the great Deisis in the south gallery of Hagia Sophia. Probably dating from soon after the Byzantine reoccupation of the city in 1261.

civic dignitaries, emperors, and others, in medieval Byzantium the tradition of making such statues appears to have effectively disappeared, although we are told that the Emperor Andronicus I (1183–5) did plan to erect a bronze statue of himself, indicating some sort of protean Comnenian revival in such sculpture.

As a result (as noted in Chapter 2) the numerous ancient statues that continued to adorn the city of Constantinople were regarded by many medieval Byzantine viewers with considerable fear and trepidation: the product of an alien age, they were often ascribed magical and prophetic powers, or treated as the abode of demons. Such views were shared even by the literate and the educated, as is revealed by a fascinating 8th-century guide to the monuments of Constantinople entitled the *Parastaseis Syntomoi Chronikai*, the author of which took a supernaturalist stance with respect to the statues in his midst. As the great scholar of Byzantine civilization, Cyril Mango, has noted, it tells one a great deal of how statues were commonly viewed in Byzantium that a standard Medieval Byzantine Greek word for them (*stoicheion*) ends up in Modern Greek meaning a ghost or 'a spirit attached to a specific place'.

Free thinkers

The survival and transmission of ancient literary and philosophical texts, and their continued study (even if, at some moments in time, only by a relatively small number of scholars) meant that Byzantine views of art, culture, and religion were never monolithic, and there were always sensitive minds capable of appreciating the ancient, elegant, or peculiar in their own terms.

In the early 13th century, for example, the contemporary historian Nicetas Choniates regarded with horror the destruction of many of the ancient statues of Constantinople by the marauding knights of the Fourth Crusade, whom he attacked as 'haters of the beautiful'. To Nicetas, these statues were not objects to be feared: rather, they were works of art whose loss was to be mourned. Thus he wrote that the statues of the sphinxes (decried by the Church) were 'like comely women in the front, and like horrible beasts in their hind parts, moving on foot in a newly invented manner, and nimbly borne aloft on their wings, rivalling the great winged birds'.

Also in the 13th century, Theodore II Lascaris (ruler of the Byzantine 'Empire' of Nicaea, which maintained an independent existence in western Asia Minor during the period of Latin rule in

Constantinople) wrote of the ancient monuments of Pergamum in terms that reveal a profound reverence for antiquity: the towers that surrounded the ancient theatre there were, he declared, 'not the work of a modern hand, nor the invention of a modern mind, for their very sight fills one with astonishment'. 'The works of the dead,' he pronounced, 'are more beautiful than those of the living'.

Throughout the history of Byzantium, such intellectual autonomy could cause problems for the Church. In the 6th and 7th centuries, for example, the practice of praying to deceased saints was challenged on the grounds that Aristotle had taught that the body and soul were mutually dependent, and that the one, therefore, could not exist without the other.

Likewise, in the 11th century, the half-Norman philosopher John Italus (a pupil of perhaps the greatest Byzantine intellectual, Michael Psellus) was banned from teaching and confined to a monastery for (among other things) having sought to apply philosophical dialectic to Christology, pagan doctrines (such as those pertaining to the eternity of the world) to cosmology, and for having advocated the reality of Platonic concepts such as the transmigration of souls. Many of John's sympathizers, one should note, were churchmen, and his condemnation bears all the hallmarks of a politically motivated show-trial, but the grounds on which he was attacked were, nevertheless, revealing.

At the very end of the Byzantine Middle Ages, the Neoplatonist scholar George Gemistos, who renamed himself Plethon (c. 1360–1452) advocated in his old age the worship of a revised form of the Greek pantheon, headed by Zeus (in spite of the fact that he himself participated in theological negotiations between the empire and the Papacy). Plethon's startling break with the religion of his birth perhaps reveals the extent to which the tensions between Christianity and Hellenism had never quite been fully resolved. Plethon had felt obliged to choose between the two, and, like the Emperor Julian before him, had ultimately chosen Hellenism.

Chapter 7
End of empire

Romans, Franks, Greeks, and Turks

The Latin sack of Constantinople in 1204 was a devastating blow to the Byzantine world from which it was never really to recover. Lurid accounts of the horrors associated with the city's fall, such as the rape of nuns, the destruction of icons, and the ransacking of churches circulated to both east and west. Much of what was not destroyed in terms of art, statuary, and holy relics was looted or sold and ended up adorning the cities of Italy (most notably the former Byzantine colony of Venice) as well as the monasteries and cathedrals of the rest of western Christendom.

Understandably, many western observers viewed the events of 1204 with considerable moral unease, and convoluted theological and providential justifications had to be concocted for the 'holy thefts' (*furta sacra*) in which the crusaders (including Latin clergy) had engaged. Equally understandably, many eastern commentators reacted by coming to view westerners with unmitigated hostility: the Latin or Frank was now increasingly cast in the role of the 'other' against whom the Byzantines defined themselves. This was especially true in terms of religious identity.

Ever since Rome had ceased to be a directly managed part of the Roman Empire, relations between Byzantium and the Bishops or

Popes of Rome had been periodically tense, and from the 8th and 9th centuries in particular the western church (headed by the Pope) and the Byzantine Church (headed by the Patriarch of Constantinople) had begun to diverge in terms of practices and customs.

The emergence of the Papacy as an autonomous political power by the 11th century had exacerbated such tensions, leading to a short-lived 'schism' between east and west in 1054. However, popes, emperors, and patriarchs had nevertheless continued to be able to work together when circumstances demanded (as the background to the First Crusade had demonstrated). After 1204, however, such cooperation would become nigh on impossible. Differences of practice increasingly hardened into disagreements over theology, focusing in particular on Latin additions to the creed. While pragmatic emperors, such as Michael VIII Palaiologos (1261–82) continued to attempt to restore ecclesiastical unity through coming to terms with the Papacy, aware that Byzantium remained both vulnerable to attack from the west and in need of Latin support against the Turks, the imperial church became less and less biddable. The very act of reaching out to the Pope was interpreted by some as an act of impiety. Orthodoxy (informed by hostility to Rome) and Byzantine identity were becoming one.

At the same time, the Latin occupation led elements within Byzantium's educated elite to reconsider the Greek aspect to their identity. The Byzantines, as we have seen, always regarded themselves (and were always regarded by their eastern neighbours) as Roman. From the 8th century onwards, however, this Roman identity had been challenged by westerners (such as the Carolingian and Ottonian emperors) who also wished to lay claim to the Roman past, and who responded by calling the Byzantines Greeks.

To the Byzantines themselves, the term Greek or 'Hellene' had traditionally served not so much as an ethnic, but rather a religious designation, meaning pagan. In the aftermath of 1204, however, one begins to find Byzantine intellectuals laying claim to the Greek identity that had been projected on to them from the outside, and appropriating it as a form of resistance to Latin intrusion and rule. A gradual process was thereby initiated whereby a Roman Orthodox identity would begin to give way to a Greek Orthodox one.

Politically, the fall of Constantinople to the crusaders had led to fragmentation, as the city's conquerors had appointed their own emperor, Baldwin of Flanders (1204–5), and their own Latin patriarch. The westerners also projected their rule over Thessalonica and its surrounding territories in northern Greece and Macedonia, and southern Greece and the Peloponnese, where Latin adventurers carved out fiefdoms of their own. Cyprus, Serbia, and Bulgaria had already fallen out of imperial control, however, and around Trebizond along the coast of the Black Sea, Nicaea in western Asia Minor, and Epirus in central and north-western Greece, autonomous Greek-speaking and Orthodox regimes emerged that laid claim to the mantle of the emperors of Constantinople the New Rome.

These Byzantine 'governments in exile' jostled for position against one another, and were never fully reintegrated into a unified Byzantine state even after Michael VIII Palaiologus had driven the Latins out of Constantinople from his base at Nicaea in 1261 and restored the semblance of empire (Latin rule having been rendered vulnerable from the start by a major defeat at the hands of the Bulgars in 1207). Thus the Empire of Trebizond (headed by a member of the Comnenian dynasty) carved out an increasingly lucrative place for itself as the main *entrepôt* at the westernmost end of the silk route, while the Empire of Epirus maintained its separate identity until it was conquered by the Serbs in the 14th century. In southern Greece and Cyprus, too, localized Latin regimes clung on, their leaders entering into increasingly symbiotic relations with local Greek-speaking elites (known as *archontes*), with whom they conspired in the exploitation of the peasantry.

Constantinople continued throughout this period to be a great centre of trade and international commerce. The proceeds of such trade, however primarily filled the pockets of foreign merchants and the Byzantine aristocracy (who increasingly entrusted their savings to bank accounts in Italy). By contrast, the political fragmentation of its territories meant that the Byzantine government was progressively impoverished, and even more dependent than before on playing off its rivals against one another to secure political survival.

In 1282, for example, in an episode known as 'the Sicilian Vespers', the Byzantine authorities sponsored an indigenous uprising and Aragonese invasion of Sicily which served to prevent Charles of Anjou, brother of the French King Louis IX (who laid claim to the Latin Empire of Constantinople) from launching a campaign of reconquest against the city. As the Frankish *Chronicle of Morea* put it, it was now 'with deceit and guile' that the Byzantines fought battles with the Franks.

It was a sign of imperial financial exhaustion that in 1343 (in the context of a civil war) the crown jewels were mortgaged to Venice (which remained a major force in the commercial life of the empire), while at some point between 1354 and 1366 the imperial government stopped minting gold coins, thereby ending a tradition that stretched back to the Emperor Constantine.

Cultural life, however, flourished. The renewed emphasis on the Greek component within Byzantine identity led to genuine intellectual engagement with the classical tradition in both literature and philosophy (as exemplified by the maverick but brilliant figure of Plethon), and for the first time a significant body of writing in Latin (from Cicero to Thomas Aquinas) was translated into Greek.

Above all, it was during the Palaiologan period that Byzantine religious art arguably reached its creative climax, combining a profound sense of the mystical, informed by contemporary trends in theology, with a novel emphasis on narrative scenes. The frescoes and mosaics that survive from the monastic church of the Chora (now the Kariye Museum in Istanbul), founded by the 14th-century statesman and scholar Theodore Metochites provide vivid testimony as to the quality of late Byzantine art, which equalled and paralleled that of contemporary Italy (see Figure 8).

It is a sign of the empire's ongoing cultural prestige that Byzantine art continued to be emulated and copied well beyond the political confines of empire, especially in the Balkans and, later, Russia, where it reached its most intense spiritualization at the hands of an artist known as Theophanes the Greek, active in Novgorod and Moscow.

As so often in the past, however, it was ultimately a reconfiguration of power on Byzantium's eastern frontier that served to determine the empire's fortunes. The ability of the Byzantine administration in Nicaea to first contain and then extirpate the Latin regime in Constantinople had been greatly aided by the relatively quiescent nature of the Seljuk Turks, with whom it had been able to negotiate relatively peaceful relations. After a manner that echoed the earlier decline of the Abbasid caliphate, however, the 13th century had witnessed a general waning of Seljuk power, as the active leadership of the *jihad* against the Christians of Rum (as the Turks knew them) passed to a series of locally based and religiously motivated marcher lords or *ghazis* ('defenders of the faith') of Turkish origin.

The autonomy of these *ghazis* had been greatly enhanced in 1243, when the Seljuks were defeated by the rapidly expanding nomad power of the Mongols, whose empire extended to embrace not only Persia but also China to the east. Now rendered tributaries of the Mongol *Ilkhan* of Persia, the Seljuk dynasty was a busted flush.

8. Mosaic depiction of Theodore Metochites offering his monastery to Christ (14th century). Kariye Museum, Istanbul.

'What dost thou now, ancient glory of Rome?'

The power vacuum caused by Seljuk decline was filled by the competing ambitions of the increasingly aggressive *ghazis* of the frontier zone, whose ability to win booty and slaves from their Christian neighbours led to a rapid accumulation of followers and prestige. In particular, from their base in north-west Anatolia, the dynasty of Osman (died *c.* 1324), Orhan (*c.* 1324–62), and Murad I (1362–89), expanded rapidly westwards against the restored Byzantine Empire and southwards and eastwards against their Turkish rivals.

Crucially, in 1354, these 'Ottoman' Turks (so-named after Osman) managed to expand their power into Europe, capturing Gallipoli before extending their control over Macedonia and Bulgaria. In a decisive encounter in 1389, the Serbian Prince Lazar was defeated at the battle of Kosovo, signalling a rapid collapse in the Christian position, and opening the way to large-scale settlement of the Balkans by Muslim Turks, who provided military service in return for landholdings. In 1396 the Turks also defeated a large crusader army that was sent against them at the battle of Nicopolis, and the Sultan Bayezid I (1389–1402) pressed on into Hungary, extending his power to the south of the Danube. Having been driven from Asia Minor, the Byzantine Empire found itself encircled.

The situation from the perspective of Constantinople was now critical. Ever since the Fourth Crusade, it had become apparent to members of the Byzantine governing classes that their empire was not in fact destined to be eternal, but rather, like all other empires, was subject not only to decay but to destruction. Indeed, in the early 14th century the statesman and scholar Theodore Metochites had admitted that very point.

Destruction now seemed imminent, however. It was a sign of how critical things were that the Emperor Manuel II Palaiologos (1391–1425) made a visit to the west to elicit aid. In Paris, he was feted by the professors of the Sorbonne and housed in the Louvre, while on Christmas Day 1400 he dined with King Henry IV of England in the palace at Eltham. Henry's courtier, Adam of Usk, noted of the event: 'I reflected how grievous it was that this great Christian prince should be driven by the Saracens from the furthest east to these furthest Western islands... O God, what dost thou now, ancient glory of Rome?'

While honourably received, Manuel received little by way of tangible support. Without ecclesiastical union with Rome, there would be no substantial military commitment from the west. Yet the legacy of the events of 1204 meant that no such union would ever be acceptable to most of the leaders of the Byzantine Church, who had learned that true religion was capable of survival whether or not an emperor sat on the throne in Constantinople. Thus, although at the Council of Florence in 1439 Manuel's successor as emperor, John VIII (1425–48), essentially conceded to western demands and accepted Papal supremacy, his capitulation was flatly rejected by the eastern bishops. His theological surrender was also denounced by the Orthodox rulers of Russia, who would eventually claim to be the true heirs of Constantine, and that their capital at Moscow was the 'Third Rome'.

Pressure on Byzantium had in fact eased slightly in the early 15th century. In 1402 the Ottomans were defeated by the Mongols at the Battle of Ankara. This reversal led to a protracted civil war between the sons of Bayezid, from which Mehmed I (1413–21) had eventually emerged triumphant, rapidly re-establishing control of the Ottoman Empire and reinitiating its expansion.

Attempting to take advantage of struggles within the Ottoman dynasty and court (but typically backing the losing side), the authorities in Constantinople again desperately attempted to negotiate survival, even acknowledging Ottoman overlordship. There was now, however, no force powerful enough to play off against the Turks. Accordingly, it was only a matter of time before a concerted effort would be made to take the city, whose hitherto impregnable land walls (the crusaders in 1204 having gained entry via Constantinople's maritime defences) were now looking increasingly vulnerable in the face of the advent of gunpowder and canon.

In the palace of the Caesars

For Byzantium, the end came with the rise to power of a young prince eager to establish his military credentials. In 1451, the Ottoman sultanate passed to the 19-year-old Mehmed II (1451–81), against whom the reigning Byzantine Emperor Constantine XI (1449–53) attempted to machinate. This provided Mehmed with a pretext for war, for which he prepared carefully by building enormous fortifications on the Bosphorus, imposing controls on maritime traffic, and gradually strangling the city. On 6 April 1453 a full-blown assault on the land walls was initiated, combined with attack from sea.

Assisted by Catalan and Italian mercenaries, Byzantine resistance was stiff, with civilians and nuns helping to ferry supplies to the troops on the walls. Turkish military pressure, however, was inexorable. Initially Mehmed and his generals threw irregulars (*bashi-bazouks*) at the walls of the city to wear down its defenders. Only as these booty-hungry adventurers (including Christian Greeks and Slavs in their number) were fought back were the regiments of Anatolian Turks and the elite Janissary corps sent in.

Eventually, a breach in the walls was established in the north-western sector near Blachernai, where the Virgin Mary had reputedly intervened against the Avars in 626. Now, however, there was to be no divine intervention. As the Ottoman troops swarmed through the walls and fanned out across the city, the Emperor Constantine XI and his entourage made a heroic last stand, throwing themselves into the *mêlée*. Contemporary sources record that the emperor's body was never found. Some claimed that he was plucked from the scene by an angel, who turned him to marble and hid him in a cave, whence he would return one day to liberate his people (Figure 9).

As Turkish flags were raised above the city, the leaders of certain outlying communities, such as those around the Church of St John of Stoudios to the south-west or the Latin traders of Galata (Pera) to the north-east, formally submitted to the Turks. These communities were allowed to escape with their property and places of worship substantially intact. As for the rest, in accordance with the rules of the *jihad*, they were given over to the rank-and-file army who were permitted to sack the city for three days, raping, slaughtering, or enslaving its inhabitants as they saw fit.

All public buildings, however, were the preserve of the Sultan Mehmed II—now accorded the title of *Fatih* or 'conqueror' (Figure 10). The great Cathedral Church of Hagia Sophia, where many of the city's inhabitants had fled for refuge, was stormed. Mehmed made his way there and declared that it should immediately be turned into a mosque. As his *muezzin* issued the Islamic declaration of faith from the pulpit, the sultan clambered on to the stripped altar to lead the prayers. After giving due thanks to Allah for his victory, Mehmed is reported to have paid a visit to the ruined halls of the old palace complex, where he whispered the words of a Persian poet: 'The spider weaves the curtains in the palace of the Caesars; the owl calls the watches in Afrasiab's towers'.

The vision of empire

The fall of Constantinople in 1453 would soon be followed by the Ottoman conquest of most of the remaining outposts of the

9. Miniature from a 16th-century Cretan copy of the *Oracles of Leo the Wise*, depicting the anticipated resurrection of Constantine XI.

10. Mehmed the Conqueror smelling a rose. From the 'Palace Albums', Hazine 2153, folio 10a.

broader Byzantine world. Trebizond, for example, was incorporated into the expanding Ottoman realm in 1461, signalling the end of the autonomous Comnenian state that had survived there since 1204. Importantly, significant numbers of Pontic Greeks were resettled in Constantinople, which Mehmed II was keen to restore to economic prosperity and which he eventually established as the capital of his now sprawling empire.

Ruling from the city of Constantine, it was perhaps inevitable that Mehmed and his successors would draw upon elements of the Byzantine political and cultural legacy. The sultan was eager to call upon the services of surviving members of the Byzantine aristocracy (although he had wiped out its leading members), and certain of his Greek-speaking courtiers, many of whom converted to Islam, accorded him the ancient imperial title of *basileus*. The Orthodox Patriarchate was restored, and the patriarch was charged with leadership over and responsibility for the sultan's Greek Orthodox subjects (thereby establishing the Church as the major vehicle for the survival of Greek identity in the centuries ahead).

Moreover, Mehmed and his heirs were determined to literally build on the achievements of the rulers of Byzantium: beneath the Topkapi palace from which they ruled, they buried the sarcophagi of Byzantine rulers, including Heraclius, whose tombs had originally been placed in the Church of the Holy Apostles, while that Church was demolished and replaced by a mosque honouring Mehmed Fatih.

Although henceforth a predominantly Muslim city, Ottoman Constantinople would nevertheless remain home to a significant Christian population. Around the offices of the Orthodox patriarch, for example, a new Greek-speaking elite of intermediaries and officials would take shape (known as 'Phanariots', after the Fanar district where the Patriarchate would come to be based). Many of these men claimed (largely spurious) Byzantine descent, and into the 18th century would continue to write Greek in the Attic style after the manner of the Second Sophistic.

Constantinople, of course, also continued to be an imperial city until the abolition of the Ottoman Empire in 1923, and Greek-speaking Christians, as well as Armenians and Jews, remained a vital element within it. Only in 1960 was the last sizeable community of Greeks driven out in a politically inspired *pogrom*.

Indeed, part of the great legacy of Byzantium would prove to be the vision of Constantinople as an imperial capital. Accordingly, as Ottoman power began to wane in the 18th and 19th centuries, neighbouring powers would eye it jealously, and competed to establish themselves there. This was particularly true of the Russian Tsars, who aspired to re-establishing Constantinople as a Christian city (in World War I, for example, a Russian imperial officer of Greek descent was even entrusted with a cross which was to be placed on top of Hagia Sophia upon the anticipated Russian capture of the city).

The dream of a restored Christian Empire ruled from Constantinople only really came to an end in 1922, when the armies of the relatively recently established Kingdom of Greece, ruled by a King Constantine, made a madly overambitious grab for territory in western Asia Minor (where large Greek-speaking communities existed), only to collapse before the forces of the Turkish commander Kemal Ataturk ('the Father of the Turks'). Ataturk drove the Greeks out, declared a republic, officially renamed Constantinople Istanbul, and moved the capital of his new state to Ankara.

Byzantium would also, of course, bequeath a cultural legacy, mediated in part by the Orthodox Church, its liturgy, art, and music, as well as through its scholars and intellectuals, many of whom had migrated to Italy to teach Greek studies long before the fall of their homeland in 1453. If the *philosophes* of the

Enlightenment would ultimately scorn the cultural and political achievement of Byzantium, they did so on the basis of an intellectual formation in the classics that owed much to the efforts of Byzantine humanists and their preservation and transmission of ancient Greek texts.

Now that the certainties of the Enlightenment seem less secure, we are perhaps in a stronger position to appreciate the richness and complexity of a civilization that lasted over a thousand years and which, as we see in the poetry of Yeats or apprehend in the music of the modern composer John Taverner, retained an ability to move and inspire long thereafter.

References

Chapter 1: What was Byzantium?

On the reception of Byzantium from the Renaissance to the Enlightenment, see G. Ostrogorsky *History of the Byzantine State* (Oxford, 1968) chapter 1.

For Themistius, see *Politics, Philosophy and Empire in the Fourth Century: Themistius' Select Orations* tr. P. Heather and D. Moncur (Liverpool, 2001).

Aurelius Victor *Liber de Caesaribus* tr. H. W. Bird (Liverpool, 1994).

C. Williams *The Arthurian Poems of Charles Williams* (Cambridge, 1982).

On Yeats, see R. Nelson 'The Byzantine Poems of W. B. Yeats' in his *Hagia Sophia 1850–1950: Holy Wisdom Modern Monument* (Chicago, 2004).

Epigraph taken from Charles Williams, *Taliessin through Logres*, with kind permission of David Higham Associates.

Chapter 2: Constantinople the ruling city

Ammianus Marcellinus *Res Gestae* tr. J. C. Role (Cambridge, MA, 1935).

A. Berger *Accounts of Medieval Constantinople: The Patria* (Cambridge, MA, 2013).

For the 'Book of the Prefect', see *Roman Law in the Later Roman Empire* tr. E. H. Freshfield (Cambridge, 1938), or J. Koder *Das Eparchenbuch Leons des Weisen* (Vienna, 1991).

Constantine Porphyrogenitus *The Book of Ceremonies* tr. A. Moffatt and M. Tall (Canberra, 2012).

P. Magdalino *Studies in the History and Topography of Byzantine Constantinople* (Aldershot, 2007).

For priapic bear, clowns, etc., see E. Maguire and H. Maguire *Other Icons: Art and Power in Byzantine Secular Culture* (Princeton, 2006).

Procopius *Secret History* tr. G. Williamson and P. Sarris (New York and London, 2007).

Procopius *History of the Wars, Secret History, Buildings* tr. H. B. Dewing and G. Downey (Cambridge, MA, 1914–40).

For statues, see S. Bassett *The Urban Image of Late Antique Constantinople* (Cambridge, 2004).

Chapter 3: From antiquity to the Middle Ages

Acts of the Council of Constantinople of 553 tr. R. Price (Liverpool, 2009).

For Islam as a 'nativist reaction', see P. Crone and M. Cook *Hagarism and the Making of the Islamic World* (Cambridge, 1977).

Chapter 4: Byzantium and Islam

Digenis Akritis: The Grottaferrata and Escorial Versions tr. E. Jeffreys (Cambridge, 2006).

For Manuel II, see *Manuel II Palaiologos: Dialoge mit einem Muslim* tr. K. Fürstel (Würzburg, 1995).

E. McGeer *Sowing the Dragon's Teeth: Byzantine Warfare in the Tenth Century* (Washington, DC, 1995).

Chapter 5: Strategies for survival

For the concept of 'Byzantine Commonwealth', see D. Obolensky *The Byzantine Commonwealth* (London, 1971).

For the concept of a Byzantine 'feudal revolution', see M. Whittow 'The Middle Byzantine Economy (600–1204)' in J. Shepard (ed.) *The Cambridge History of the Byzantine Empire* (Cambridge, 2008), and P. Sarris 'Large Estates and the Peasantry in Byzantium', *Revue Belge de Philologie et d'Histoire* 90 (2012).

The Complete Works of Liudprand of Cremona tr. P. Squatriti (Washington, DC, 2007).

Constantine Porphyrogenitus *De Adminstrando Imperio* tr. R. J. H. Jenkins (Washington, DC, 1967).

Anna Komnene *The Alexiad* tr. E. R. A Sewter and P. Frankopan
(London and New York, 2009).
The Strategikon of the Emperor Maurice tr. G. T. Dennis
(Philadelphia, 1984).

Chapter 6: Text, image, space, and spirit

Agathias *Histories* tr. J. D. Frendo (Berlin, 1975).
Athanasius *The Life of Antony and the Letter to Marcellinus* tr.
R. C. Gregg (Mahwah, 1979).
A. Cameron and J. Herrin *Constantinople in the Early Eighth
Century: The Parastaseis Syntomoi Chronikai* (Leiden, 1984).
The Chronicle of John Malalas tr. E. Jeffreys, M. Jeffreys, and R. Scott
(Melbourne, 1986).
For the Church and visual culture, see E. Maguire and H. Maguire
Other Icons: Art and Power in Byzantine Secular Culture
(Princeton, 2006).
For Cosmas, see *La Topographie Chrétienne de Cosmas Indicopleuste*
tr. W. Wolska-Conus (Paris, 1968–73).
For 'distorting mirror', see C. Mango 'Byzantine Literature as
Distorting Mirror' in M. Mullett (ed.) *Byzantium and the Classical
Tradition* (Birmingham, 1981).
For the library of Cecaumenos, see C. Mango *Byzantium: The Empire
of New Rome* (London, 1983), chapters 6 and 13.
O City of Byzantium! Annals of Niketas Choniates tr. H. J. Magoulias
(Michigan, 1984).
Photius *The Bibliotheca* tr. N. Wilson (London, 1994).
Procopius *The Secret History* tr. G. A. Williamson and P. Sarris
(London, 2007)—includes discussion of his other works.
For responses to statues, see E. Maguire and H. Maguire *Other Icons:
Art and Power in Byzantine Secular Culture* (Princeton, 2006),
and C. Mango 'Antique Statuary and the Byzantine Beholder',
Dumbarton Oaks Papers 17 (1963).
For Romanos and the development of Byzantine verse, see
C. A. Trypanis *The Penguin Book of Greek Verse* (New York and
London, 1971).
Theophylact Simocatta *History* tr. M. and M. Whitby (Oxford, 1985).
St Basil on the Value of Greek Literature ed. N. Wilson (London, 1975).
The Works of the Emperor Julian tr. W. C. Wright (Cambridge, MA,
1913).

Chapter 7: End of empire

For Byzantine influences on the music of John Tavener, listen, for
example, to his *Two Hymns to the Mother of God* (1985).

On Manuell II in the West and Mehmed II in Constantinople, see
S. Runciman *The Fall of Constantinople 1453* (Cambridge, 1965).

Further reading

General

M. Angold *Byzantium: The Bridge from Antiquity to the Middle Ages* (2001).
A. Cameron *Byzantine Matters* (Princeton, 2014).
A. Cameron *The Byzantines* (New York, 2009).
C. Mango *Byzantium: The Empire of New Rome* (London, 1983).
C. Mango *The Oxford History of Byzantium* (Oxford, 2002).
J. Shepard (ed.) *The Cambridge History of the Byzantine Empire c.500–1492* (Cambridge, 2008).

Chapter 1: What was Byzantium?

J. Bardill *Constantine: Divine Emperor of the Christian Golden Age* (Cambridge, 2012).
T. D. Barnes *Constantine: Dynasty, Religion and Power in the Later Roman Empire* (New York, 2010).
P. Brown *The World of Late Antiquity* (London, 1971).
P. Stephenson *Constantine: Unconquered Emperor, Christian Victor* (London, 2009).

Chapter 2: Constantinople the ruling city

S. Bassett *The Urban Image of Late Antique Constantinople* (Cambridge, 2004).
J. Harris *Constantinople: Capital of Byzantium* (London, 2007).

P. Magdalino *Studies in the History and Topography of Byzantine Constantinople* (Aldershot, 2007).

C. Mango *Byzantine Architecture* (London, 1986).

C. Mango *Le développement urbain de Constantinople* (Paris, 1985).

Chapter 3: From antiquity to the Middle Ages

A. Cameron *The Mediterranean World in Late Antiquity, c.395–700* (London, 2011).

G. Dagron *Emperor and Priest: The Imperial Office in Byzantium* (Cambridge, 2003).

J. Haldon *Byzantium in the Seventh Century: The Transformation of a Culture* (Cambridge, 1993).

J. Howard-Johnston *Witnesses to a World Crisis* (Oxford, 2010).

P. Sarris *Empires of Faith: The Fall of Rome to the Rise of Islam* (Oxford, 2011).

Chapter 4: Byzantium and Islam

L. Brubaker and J. Haldon *Byzantium in the Iconoclast Era, c.680–850, A History* (Cambridge, 2010).

R. Hoyland *Seeing Islam As Others Saw It* (Princeton, 1997).

C. Robinson (ed.) *The New Cambridge History of Islam, Volume One: The Formation of the Islamic World, Sixth to Eleventh Centuries* (Cambridge, 2011).

I. Shahid *Byzantium and the Arabs in the Fifth Century* (Washington, DC, 1989).

Chapter 5: Strategies for survival

M. Angold *The Byzantine Empire 1025–1204* (London, 1984).

P. Frankopan *The First Crusade: The Call From the East* (London, 2012).

C. Holmes *Basil II and the Governance of Empire* (Oxford, 2005).

P. Magdalino *The Empire of Manuel I Komnenos, 1143–1190* (Cambridge, 1991).

D. Obolensky *The Byzantine Commonwealth* (London, 1971).

J. Shepard and S. Franklin *Byzantine Diplomacy* (Aldershot, 1992).

P. Stephenson *Byzantium's Balkan Frontier: A Political Study of the Northern Balkans 900–1204* (Cambridge, 2006).

M. Whittow *The Making of Orthodox Byzantium* (London, 1996).

Chapter 6: Text, image, space, and spirit

J. Baun *Tales From Another Byzantium: Celestial Journey and Local Community in the Medieval Greek Apocrypha* (Cambridge, 2007).

R. Cormack *Byzantine Art* (Oxford, 2000).

A. Kaldellis *Hellenism in Byzantium* (Cambridge, 2007).

P. Lemerle *Byzantine Humanism* (Canberra, 1987).

R. Macrides (ed.) *History as Literature in Byzantium* (Aldershot, 2010).

E. Maguire and H. Maguire *Other Icons: Art and Power in Byzantine Secular Culture* (Princeton, 2006).

C. Mango *The Art of the Byzantine Empire 312–1453* (Toronto, 1986).

C. Mango *Byzantine Architecture* (Milan, 1986).

C. Mango *Byzantium: The Empire of New Rome* (Oxford, 1983).

Chapter 7: End of empire

A. T. Aftonomos *The Stream of Time Irresistible: Byzantine Civilisation in the Modern Popular Imagination* (Montreal, 2005).

D. Angelov *Imperial Ideology and Political Thought in Byzantium 1204–1430* (Cambridge, 2009).

M. Angold *A Byzantine Government in Exile: Government and Society Under the Laskarids of Nicaea 1204–61* (Oxford, 1975).

M. Angold *The Fall of Constantinople to the Ottomans* (London, 2012).

J. Harris *The End of Byzantium* (New Haven, 2010).

J. Harris, C. Holmes, and E. Russell (eds) *Byzantines, Latins and Turks in the Eastern Mediterranean World After 1150* (Oxford, 2012).

H. Inalcik *The Ottoman Empire: The Classical Age 1300–1600* (London, 1973).

P. Mansel *Constantinople: City of the World's Desire, 1453–1924* (London, 1995).

G. Page *Being Byzantine: Greek Identity before the Ottomans* (Cambridge, 2008).

S. Runciman *Byzantine Style and Civilization* (Cambridge, 1975).

S. Runciman *The Fall of Constantinople 1453* (Cambridge, 1965).

T. Shawcross *The Chronicle of Morea: Historiography in Crusader Greece* (Oxford, 2009).

K. Ware *The Orthodox Way* (Mowbray, 1979).

Index

Expand your collection of
VERY SHORT INTRODUCTIONS